TIME
MILLIONAIRE

CREATE MORE TIME FOR THE THINGS YOU LOVE
WITH THE ULTIMATE SIDE HUSTLE

ANGIE GARNER
#HUSTLESMARTER

Interior design by IDA FIA SVENINGSSON and JEN HENDERSON
Cover design by IDA FIA SVENINGSSON

Print ISBN: 978-0-692-11343-1

DEDICATION

For Sweet Jamesy.

My greatest joy is spending quality time with you.

CONTENTS

TIME MILLIONAIRE?

Every Friday morning around 9:30 a.m. I take my sweet time relaxing in the sauna and steam room, and then I hit the pool for some laps. At this point in the day, the morning rush is gone and I am sharing lanes with the 65+ crowd. Just me and the retirees. The way I like it.

As a Time Millionaire, in many ways I live my life in contrast to the majority. I grocery shop at 10am on Tuesdays and don't have to fight my way through crowded aisles. I take long vacations in May and don't have to pay peak travel prices. I love Mondays, because a Monday is no different than a Friday in my world. James and I leave for "weekend" getaways on Wednesdays, putting us the opposite direction of traffic. A true commodity in the Seattle-area.

A Time Millionaire has the final say in how they spend the 24 hours they are gifted with each and every day. A Time Millionaire is not limited by the "9-5" dictated by most corporations. A Time Millionaire does not have to ask permission to miss a workday and is not allotted a set amount of vacation time. A Time Millionaire is wealthy with options regarding what they do and who they spend time with. A Time Millionaire is living a "freedom-based lifestyle."

There are several terms I will use throughout this book that I want to clearly define for you:

99 Freedom-based lifestyle

Living a freedom-based lifestyle means you have the ability to determine the course of your daily schedule and overall life direction. You don't have a boss, and you can never get fired. Your success (however you define it) is completely dependent on your own effort and timeline. You are granted creative independence and the option to choose when you want to work on your business, and when you want to block off your schedule for family time. Essentially, you get to wake up every day and choose your own adventure.

99 Residual income

Also commonly called "passive" income, residual income is when you continue to get paid after the work is done. The key idea here is leverage. Leveraging other people's time or other people's money creates a residual income. Residual income allows you to make money while you're on vacation, while you're spending quality time with your family, and even while you're sleeping.

🙼 Direct sales

Direct selling is a retail channel in which independent distributors market and sell products directly to the consumer without the need for a physical storefront, thus breaking away from the costly, generic retail tradition. Direct selling consultants work on their own, but affiliate with a company that uses this channel, retaining the freedom to run a business on their own terms. I will also refer to this business model as "network marketing" and "multi-level marketing" (MLM).

🙼 Side hustle

A side hustle is a way to earn extra "Plan B" income that allows flexibility to pay off debt and/or enrich your lifestyle. It can also be your opportunity to delve into whatever you are most passionate about without quitting your full-time job.

INTRODUCTION

The Skinny Dip

One morning during my travels in one of the more rural corners of the world, I awoke to the neighborhood rooster cock-a-doodle-dooing. I could hear birds singing sweet chirps and dogs barking in the distance, but beyond that, only silence. Sweet Jamesy was happily dozing to the right of me, his lips curled up into a smile. Typical. I kissed his forehead and basked in his peacefulness. Eventually, I escaped the grasp of the white, fluffy covers, walked up to the double-pane window, and thrust open the shutters. A bright October day welcomed me. Deep breath in...ahhhh. The unparalleled aroma of bougainvillea and salty ocean consumed my every fiber.

I walked down the stairs and out to the back porch of the modern-rustic villa where I was greeted by Niko Suave, our orangey adopted stray cat for the week. He rubbed my ankles almost as if he could guess the meaning of this day. Or he could sense the cat food on the kitchen counter. I patted his head, stripped down to my birthday suit, and jumped into the infinity pool overlooking the Ionian Sea.

Turning 30 never felt so good.

———————

It had always been my goal to be a millionaire by the age of 30. Being a millionaire represented *freedom*. Freedom to give, save, invest, and bless. Freedom to live where I wanted, eat what I wanted, and go where I wanted. Freedom from arguing with my spouse, friends, and family about money. Freedom to start businesses; businesses that would add significance to the world. Freedom to experience the fullness of life.

As I folded my arms and leaned against the edge of the pool to gawk at the sweeping cliffside view in all of my natural glory, I reflected on the incredible fulfilled dreams that lead me to this exact beautiful moment. Even though I wasn't yet a millionaire, what I had was more precious than diamonds: TIME. I was a Time Millionaire. I was debt-free after paying off $95,000 in business loans and back taxes. I no longer had to work as a personal trainer because I had partnered with a direct sales company and replaced my income by building a true business. And now, with Sweet Jamesy by my side, I was traveling around the world; sixteen countries and five continents over eight months for #GarnersGoGlobal. We were actually living the "Four Hour Work Week," something we had been talking about since our very first date on a hot summer's night under a towering madrona tree.

Tired hair stylists, retail workers, and salespeople, I see you. Overwhelmed lawyers, trainers, servers, and teachers, I feel you. Entrepreneur hopefuls and those who want to change the world, I hear you crying out for time to be with your family; time to pour yourself into your passions and hobbies; time to travel, to create, to connect, to sleep soundly, and to enjoy all that is sweet in life.

The common belief is that you have to choose between money and time, but I'm here to tell you: you can *absolutely* have both.

Defining Moment

"I'm going into labor!"

My heart dropped to the depths of my chest. I was going to miss it. Worse, I was choosing to miss it. It was a Saturday morning, and I was booked with clients back-to-back. Five sessions, to be exact, representing $325 of income. I was barely hanging on financially, and I needed that money for rent. However, my sister wanted me by her side when she was giving birth to my niece down in Vancouver, about three hours south of Seattle. She had told me a week prior how much it would mean to her. I felt trapped. Even though I was running a personal training business and could have easily rescheduled with little backlash, I had no other way to make up that $325. I had to stay.

I stayed, and I missed out on an irreplaceable memory. That was a defining moment for me because it forced me to take a hard look at reality: I didn't actually own a business. My business owned me. If I didn't work, I didn't get paid. If clients were sick, I didn't get paid. If clients went on vacation, I didn't get paid. If I went on vacation, I didn't get paid, and I had to pay for the vacation. So I didn't ever go on vacation...and I like vacations!

Even though there was a business license with my name on it, I was a "fakepreneur." There was no duplication and no systems in place. I was eternally grateful for my clients, but the gig itself was a ball and chain. I continually said yes to being at the gym at certain hours and on days I didn't prefer to. I was on a serious steady drip of caffeine to maintain enthusiasm for 12-hour workdays. I trained six days per week with one day left for errands and laundry. I desperately wanted to spend more quality time with my super-hottie new boyfriend, James. I wished so badly I could work out on my own at the times I wanted to, and maybe just maybe, I could sleep in without an alarm clock chiming at the crack of dawn. More often than not, my 8 p.m. client would walk in and, as delightful as they were, I was absolutely wiped and had to retreat to the bathroom for a pep talk with myself in the mirror: "You can do this, Angie! Pull it together! They deserve your best just like your 8 a.m.

client got from you." There was no way I was going to be doing this when I turned 30, I told myself. Something had to change.

MIRACLES HAPPEN WHEN *MAYBES* BECOME *WILLS*, *SHOULDS* BECOME *MUSTS*, AND *COULDS* BECOME COMMITMENTS.

There is so much blessing on the other side of definitive action, and I knew that if I didn't intentionally make a change, nothing would *ever* change. That resolve allowed me to let down my guard and seriously consider the options available to me.

And there it was...staring at me on the kitchen counter.

Redefining Retirement

Retirement is generally thought of as a permanent vacation. *Arrivederci*, responsibility! Cash flow is on autopilot. Not a care in the world. Just kick back on that beach chair, sip a fruity drink with a little umbrella in it, and read People magazine while you wait for your daily massage in the outdoor cabana.

In case you've never done this for a few days in a row before, let me ease your fear of missing out (FOMO): it gets old reeeeeal fast. Sure, I love the occasional sun bronzing margarita session, but I will never, ever stop working. We are designed to work. Work is satisfying. Work is honorable. Work gets you out of bed in the morning with healthy determination. Work fuels the insatiable desire to create.

But, there's a big difference between work that's chosen for you and work you choose to do.

Here's how I define retirement: living off a residual income stream with the time and freedom to do what you want, with whom you want, wherever you want. If you want to design a life you love, you absolutely can. You do it by earning your time freedom through growing a business that pays you while you're sleeping and doesn't require 40-plus hour workweeks. Then you are able to leverage your abundant time to continue making an impact on your family and the community. You are free to create, to connect, to explore, to inspire, and to give.

My goal is to help you not just get by in life, but to build a residual income stream so you can spend abundant time with loved ones and contribute your gifts to the world.

Building a Plan-B income isn't only extremely wise, it is becoming increasingly necessary to keep up with the rising cost of living and the unpredictability of the economy. Since the recession of 2008, we have transformed into a "gig economy" as employees are looking for more monetary security with a second source of income. Also, if you have student loans that contribute to the $1.4 trillion dollars of student loan debt in our nation, there isn't going to be a bailout program for you, either. The best way to get free is to increase your income, and there's no better way than with the ultimate side hustle.

After that defining moment missing the birth of my niece, I made a decision to stop running from the best opportunity I had in front of me: network marketing. Getting rich overnight doesn't exist, but network marketing does provide a fast track to building wealth. It does not require you to be super tech-savvy or have loads of dough to invest. No need for venture capital, Whitney Houston-esque pipes, or even a brilliant idea. It doesn't require office space, employees, or Mark Zuckerberg-ish smarts to be wildly successful. And the possible return on investment? It can be legacy changing.

Time Millionaire **walks you through the process of choosing a direct sales business opportunity that aligns with your values and vision without taking away from your family or full-time job.**

Chapter 1 helps you define *why* you want to build a side hustle in the first place. You will learn how to live with passion by uncovering your purpose and calling while energizing your natural gifts. Chapters 2 and 3 are dedicated to helping you define *who* you need to become to run a successful business. In Chapter 2, you will identify habits needed to take your confidence and self-esteem to an entirely new level. Chapter 3 will reveal areas where your mindset may need to be expanded in order to get the success you're after, especially in regards to money and fear. Chapter 4 is the *what* behind the ultimate side hustle. By the end of this chapter, you will understand the business model of network marketing and all lingering questions you may have about how it works will be answered. Chapters 5, 6 and 7 are designed to teach you *how* to actually get your business off the ground. Chapter 5 takes you through my annual goal setting process so you can crystalize your vision. Chapter 6 narrows in on the skills you must develop to take your business as far as you want, and Chapter 7 outlines the exact steps to grow yourself personally while getting your business into orbit.

By the end of this book, you will be absolutely certain as to whether or not direct sales is for you, and you will learn countless success principles along the way.

I cover so many ideas throughout this book that, quite frankly, each section could be a book on its own. Instead of extensively focusing on just one or two points, I went very wide with an array of teaching. Take your time reading each section and truly reflecting. Essentially, _Time Millionaire_ is a manual for someone who is being introduced to the idea of thinking like an entrepreneur and personally growing to see a dream realized. It is absolutely packed with applicable tools to increase your mindset and belief.

To help you navigate your thoughts and put action behind what you are learning, I have included _Reflection Sections_ throughout the chapters. I urge you to invest into a brand new journal and take the time to write your answers to these questions and promptings as you read the book. To make this even easier, I have included a totally free downloadable PDF with all of the _Reflection Sections_ in one spot.

To download the free workbook, go to

www.timemillionairebook.com/download

It's time to imagine a better lifestyle and put in the smart hustle to see it become reality. That hustle begins with a commitment to read this book in its entirety and complete each exercise thoughtfully.

As Jim Rohn said, "I'm working full-time on my job and part time on my fortune. But it won't be long before I'm working full-time on my fortune. Can you imagine what my life will look like?"

LET'S GET TO WORK!

Life is too short to be too busy for what matters most.

CHAPTER 1

UNCOVER YOUR CALLING

Uncomplicate with Why

Writing this book was really complicated for me...until it wasn't. Let me explain.

The journey to write *Time Millionaire* started with a proclamation: "In 2017, I will write and self-publish my first book!"

But first, what would the book be about? What should I title the book? Who would enjoy reading this book...besides my mom? Should I talk about God? Or about money? God and money? I didn't want to come off as one of those wacky prosperity gospel ladies with poufy hair and magenta lipstick on cable television. Was the great philosopher Kanye spitting truth? "If I talk about God, my records won't get played, huh..." Hmm. Perhaps I could talk about marriage. Oh, how I love marriage. But, no, that didn't seem like the right first book. What about fitness? I've got over a decade of experience helping people get super fit and healthy.

Nah, I just wasn't feeling compelled to write about shredded abs at the moment.

Morning after morning, I would Spark™ it up and force myself to sit in front of my computer screen at 6 a.m. hoping for the inspiration to begin composing a masterpiece. Sometimes words happened; whole paragraphs, even. But more often than not, I found myself checking emails and Facebook. So, I decided upon a self-imposing restriction, and I completely disconnected from Wi-Fi. That strategy worked for about 3.7 minutes until I needed to Google a synonym and instead found myself scrolling to see how many likes my last post got. But my obsession with checking online correspondence was not the real problem (*ahem*). The problem was I spent EIGHT MONTHS attempting to write this book without genuinely uncovering why I was writing it.

I had to make a decision. Why did I feel compelled to write a book and *why* am I writing this book? Your life at this very moment is a result of your decisions. Making good decisions isn't hard when you actually take the time to uncover and commit to what you really want and, most importantly, *why* you want it. So, in January 2017, I decided I was going to write a book, and in September 2017, I finally uncovered why I was writing said book, and wouldn't you know it, I began to make real headway on a rough draft.

The power of the written word was exposed to me in 2010 when I took my first stab at writing and started a blog, "In My Spandex." This online diary chronicled my adventures as an early twenty-something, single, fabulously fit entrepreneur. I wondered who would ever be interested in my day-to-day as I pranced around in lycra while pushing heavy weights and batting my eyes at fellow meatheads in the gym. Regardless, I felt a nudge to share it with the world. It was a gut feeling, if you will. Still, who would have time in their busy day to read such nonsense?

Apparently, a lot of people. Thousands of readers enjoyed hearing about me in my spandex. They seemed to be fascinated by the love story unfolding between me and "Luke" (James' pen name). They loved the realness, the rawness, the openness, the weirdness. Many still remember that blog and have shared stories of how it helped them navigate decisions in their own lives.

Books have changed my life more than any other resource on the planet. Books open the doors to conversations and thoughts that otherwise might not happen. Authors have the power to breathe life into your unrealized dreams, your true worth. Words on paper can transform your thinking and, in turn, transform your life.

I wrote this book because I don't want money to tear you and your spouse apart. I don't want a lack of resources to keep you from an extraordinary life. With every word, I'm fighting to help you uncover your next steps to build a business that will fund your wildest dreams. I wrote this book because I believe life is precious, and we are called to use our gifts and talents to make a difference. I wrote this book because I believe the majority of people still have a misconception about what direct sales really is and are too quick to rule it out as a viable option. I feel like I'm sitting on a secret treasure chest, and I'm bursting to share it with you.

My purpose for this book is to teach you how to free up your time with the powerful vehicle of network marketing so that you can go out into your community and be a change agent, specifically by spending more time on stuff that impacts the world at large.

I hope to serve you by teaching you how to become the best version of yourself so you can live your own epic story.

I know you might be thinking, "Angie, can we just get to the part where I learn how to make money while I sleep so I can live an incredible life with less worry, less overwhelm; more joy and more freedom?" I promise, I will show you the way. But before we get into the "how-to's" of building the ultimate side hustle, we must get crystal clear on why it even matters to you in the first place.

Why do you want more time? Do you want the freedom to create your days and make memories with your family?

Why do you want more money? Do you want to travel more, or pay off debt faster?

Why are you thinking about starting a side hustle? Do you value autonomy and want to work for yourself?

PURPOSE IS THE REASON *WHY* SOMETHING IS DONE, CREATED, OR DESIGNED. YOUR PURPOSE IS YOUR *WHY*.

Once you uncover your purpose behind a specific project, the path becomes all the clearer. You still won't likely know how everything is going to unfold, but you will certainly be able to identify your very next step.

And that's exactly how big things happen: by taking the next step.

REFLECTION SECTION

OK, it's time for an exercise. (Don't worry, it is a mental exercise, so no headstands or deadlifts required! Yay!) Any time you see *"Reflection Section"* it means I want you to open your journal and spend time reflecting and responding to the promptings. Remember, I have provided a FREE DOWNLOAD with all of the *Reflection Sections* from this book. You can download that here: **www.timemillionairebook.com/download**

The answers to the questions below will help uncover why it is urgent you become a Time Millionaire.

- What would you do with an extra $500 per month? How would that ease financial pressures in your home?
- What about an extra $5,000 per month? How would that change your current lifestyle?
- What about an extra $50,000 per month? How would you live and what would you do with your abundant money and time?

Start allowing yourself to dream about the reality of financial and time freedom and what that would do for your future and family.

The What to Your Why

Purpose is the *why* behind a specific project. But just knowing why is not enough to propel you into action. Purpose needs fuel and that comes in the form of passion. Passion is the *what* to your *why*. It's what you're obsessed with right now. It's an intense burning desire, or enthusiasm, for something.

The first time I remember being passionate about something—like, really passionate about something—was in the third grade. That something was Danny J.

I couldn't stop thinking about his soft brown eyes and bowl cut hair. I wore a new dress every single day and pranced by his desk in my Spice Girl-inspired platform heels. He seemed more into his baseball cards, but I didn't let that deter my focus. I started shaving my legs. Then I really approached next-level creeper status: I made a scrapbook all about him. I blew up his school picture from the yearbook and made that the cover. I saved pencils he dropped and papers he wrote on. I loved his boyish scribbles. One time I stole his hat, but it didn't fit in the scrapbook, so I smelled it and gave it back. He lived in a nearby neighborhood, and after school, I would knock on his door and run away. I would call him and hang up if he answered. Twenty years later, I can still remember each digit of his home phone number. Although I was too nervous to say a word to him, I was relentless in my pursuit. It did not work out between us, but this level of fearless intensity became the way I started approaching everything I was passionate about in life. Besides scaring off a few boys (OK, a *lot* of boys), it has served me well.

Because I became obsessed with my vision of freedom, I started living a lifestyle at the age of 29 that most people think is only available to them after they slog through 22-plus years in the system and another 35-plus years paying their corporate dues to "The Man."

And I'm not talking about the Maserati in the garage or the luxury world travel. Those experiences are pleasant, but they have never, ever been my driving force. What drives me is the urgency to use my short amount of time on this planet to make a difference.

Some days I like to create, some days I like to explore, some days I like to inspire, and some days I like to connect. Some days I like to meet my girlfriend at the spa and drink champagne out of plastic cups in the hot tub...on a Tuesday...at noon. To design this freedom-based lifestyle, I had to become wildly passionate about living a life of impact through the power of direct sales. And now I'm passionate about helping others do the same.

The first time the entrepreneurship bug hit me, it hit me harder than food poisoning in Morocco, which is really saying something because I genuinely thought I was going to die from eating eggplant.

Creating something that didn't exist was exciting. My passion fire was lit. Just thinking about bringing a business into the world kept me up at night for weeks, similar to when I first started dating Jamesy and I couldn't sleep because I was so entranced envisioning our fairy-tale future together. My first business idea was to open a food truck. (This was before food trucks were trendy, *mmkay?*) Three friends and I were going to sell crepes to the late-night party crowd in Belltown, a neighborhood in Seattle known for midnight-hour shenanigans. "Holy Crepes" was what we were going to call it. We wrote out the menu and designed a logo. We experimented with recipes and plotted our delivery: my Indonesian goddess of a friend and I were going to dress like heavenly angels. People would eat nutella banana crepes out of the palm of our holy hands.

When we were faced with permit issues and a paperwork legal battle with the city, all four of us retreated...just like that. We weren't passionate about crepes enough to overcome the opposition. Plus, I started imagining being out in the Seattle drizzle every weekend until 3 a.m. dressed in a costume, and I'm a morning person. It would have never worked.

THERE IS NO SHORTAGE OF IDEAS; MANY PEOPLE HAVE IDEAS. THE HANG-UP IS IN THE DOING. FEW PEOPLE TAKE ACTION, AND ACTION IS FUELED BY *PASSION*.

Passion fuels motivation. Because my friends and I weren't truly passionate about fulfilling the need of late-night crepe cravings, we weren't motivated to fight. We weren't keen on persevering through adversity. We weren't willing to do the work. So, passion is clearly a crucial part of the productivity equation. But here's the tricky part with passion: it can come and go, making it an unreliable source to base all of your decisions on.

The Problem with Passion

"Do what you love and you'll never work a day in your life" is a mantra I'm sure we've all heard before, but I believe it to be misleading. It has convinced many people they will only be happy if they earn income doing that *one thing* they are passionate about. The truth is, there's no such thing as some passionate activity that you will never get tired of, never stress out about, never complain about. It doesn't exist. I am living my dream lifestyle making money doing things I love, and I still strongly dislike doing certain aspects of my business. The other reality is, passions evolve throughout life. My own path has been a series of diverse enthusiastic stepping-stones.

I've been passionate about *Star Wars*, Ricky Martin, Michael Jackson, bodybuilding, and Jesus...in that order. I started a personal training business in college that led to opening a gym that led to being more broke at 25 than I was at 20. Following my passion for fitness was not giving me time or financial freedom, so after three years of taking nutritional products from a direct sales company, I made an intentional shift to utilize the business opportunity and started coaching as an independent distributor for this company.

Leading up to this decision, I was a huge fan of the products but continued to say no to the opportunity. *Network marketing is NOT my passion,* I thought to myself. Never in a million years did I imagine selling vitamins for a living. The company did not start out as my "passion," per se, but here's what I finally realized: if I ran with this vehicle, I would have the time and energy to fund ALL of my passions.

I'm passionate about my marriage. Jamesy and I spend more quality time together than 98.2 percent of married couples in America. I made that statistic up, but I'm fairly certain of it. I'm passionate about fitness. I get to work out whenever and wherever I want, because I have four gym memberships right now. A bit excessive, I know. I'm trying to cut back. I'm passionate about family. I hopped in the car on a whim just this week to drive three hours south to visit my Dad, as he was ill and sounded lonely. We did nothing but watch home movies and eat tacos, and it was incredibly affirming to know that I had the freedom to be there for him when he needed me. I'm passionate about teaching people how to take action on their dreams, which is exactly why I'm writing this book.

Passions have their season, and because you picked up _Time Millionaire_ it is likely you are in season where you need more time, making it necessary for you to become obsessed with doing whatever it takes to create a freedom-based lifestyle.

Fund Your Passion

To become a Time Millionaire, you need to become crazy passionate about helping people and designing your life. By doing so, you will also likely free up more financial resources to make a difference. And sometimes, this process reveals completely new passions that never even existed before. That is what happened for my friend and teammate, Stephanie.

She was going about life just fine. Bills were getting paid, food was on the table, husband and kids were happy. What wasn't fine, however, was the extra twenty pounds she was holding onto after having two babies, so she committed to working with me on our company's nutrition jumpstart and took care of that pesky "baby weight." Her story started gaining attention from friends and family, and before she knew it, she had a part-time business on her hands. She began to fall in love with the process of walking people through transformation, helping them unveil health and confidence like never before. This newfound passion for wellness, combined with the extra earnings from her unexpected direct sales business, recently funded a huge dream: she opened a gym in her town where she now serves her community on an entirely new level. She paid cash to launch the dream, and it has been profitable since day one.

There are so many incredible stories of people who have funded their passions with the ultimate side hustle. A leader on our team is passionate about ministry, so she funded a missions trip to Africa with her extra income. A couple with a heart for their community paid for several low-income kids in their town to get braces. A local teammate was recently diagnosed with cancer, and because she is a Time Millionaire she didn't have to ask a boss for time off to undergo treatment. Her passion is her family, and she gets to be with them every day. Another couple in our organization is passionate about giving; they just gave away one of their extra houses to a local church. All $2.5 million of it.

When you build residual income, it gives you an abundance of money and time allowing you to pour energy and resources into whatever it is you are most passionate about.

Give yourself permission to become obsessed with doing whatever it takes to earn a freedom-based lifestyle and soon enough you will have everything you need to indulge your other passions.

 REFLECTION SECTION

What passions have you been forced to put aside in order to pay the bills? What would it feel like if you could fuel your passions on a regular basis because of all your free time as a Time Millionaire?

What's Your Wow?

You have your purpose and you are passionate about getting free. Now, the question is...*how*? How do you, with your own individual strengths and talents, work with your why in mind while helping others along the way? You do it with your *wow*.

Several years ago, despite the luxury high-rise roof over my head, the brand new cars in the garage, and the doting husband by my side, I felt an incredible discontentment. Something was missing. I wasn't waking up with a healthy anticipation for the day ahead. I sunk criss-cross applesauce into our distressed leather couch and asked myself, "What is something I love doing so much that I forget to eat when I'm doing it?"

In my journal, the answer came to me almost instantaneously: writing. I was born to be a messenger. Words of encouragement are my gift. Through writing, speaking, coaching, and singing, I am here to use my voice to cast vision and hope for people's lives. Yet, I had become so focused on my financial goals that I hadn't created any space for my gift to flourish. A dark cloud had settled over me, leaving me with a sense of emptiness.

Within days I had started an email list and was writing regularly. It nourished my soul and pulled me out of the funk.

YOUR WOW IS YOUR UNIQUE GIFT, AND YOUR GIFT IS YOUR OXYGEN. IT FLOODS YOU WITH SIGNIFICANCE AS IT FORCES YOU TO THINK OF OTHERS.

Think of your gift as your tool. It's what you do and how you do it. It is your unique way of contributing and helping others. When you use your gift, it should bring you deep satisfaction unlike anything else in your life.

If you are a creative person like me, you know how empty life feels when you aren't pouring yourself into an inspired work of art that you can share with others. No first-class trip to Hawaii will fill the void. Ignoring the call on your life to share your gift by distracting yourself with the instant gratification of booking a trip, diving into a wood-fired pizza, or buying a pair of Prada shoes will only put a Band-Aid on the problem.

You have a wow and it is your tool for making a difference as well as building your business.

 REFLECTION SECTION

Not sure what your unique gift is? Here are a few questions to bring your gift to light.

- When was the last time you lost track of time? What were you doing?
- What do people always say you are great at?
- What is something you always wish you had more time for?
- What do you feel you are the absolute best at?
- What do people come to you for help with?

Stop Stealing

Your gift is the *how* behind your *why*. It is your outlet for fulfilling your purpose behind a certain project, in turn fueling your deepest passions.

As I mentioned, the reason why I'm writing this book is to teach you how to fulfill your dreams with the power of residual income provided by the ultimate side hustle. I'm passionate about helping people, and my gift is my voice. Are you starting to see how purpose, passion and gifts are woven together to create a beautiful melody of meaning? You must have all three to find this flow, so it is imperative you discover and share your gift. I learned this long and hard way.

For many, many years, I hid my gift. I would wait until the entire family was out of the house, and then I would finally sit at the grand piano and play to my heart's content. Sometimes I was so into the chords and arpeggios that I wouldn't hear the garage door open and was terribly embarrassed when someone got home and caught a glimpse of the music I was writing and words I was singing. I would tiptoe down to the basement, put on headphones, and compose music on the keyboard when everyone was sleeping. I would hide the lyrics I had written to my songs. I would lock myself in my bedroom and watch live performances of pop superstars like Janet Jackson and Britney Spears to teach myself how to dance. I demanded that nobody walk in if my music was on, and the few times it happened as I was popping and locking in front of the mirror, I was mortified.

I didn't want to be exposed.

I feared rejection for three reasons: 1) I didn't know if I was "good enough" in comparison to the inarguable talent of my siblings; 2) if I was "good enough," I didn't want to feel like I was showing off or trying to garner attention; and 3) many of the songs I was writing were about love and Jesus, and they were very personal for a 12-year-old. I thought maybe I was just silly for writing about such intimate things.

Through massive amounts of healing from deep scars formed as I was teased in my youth, I've entered a new space in my life. A space where I am no longer concerned with being "good enough". Or overly emotional. I AM too much! And I am unapologetic about that.

Could it be that you are just as fearful of vulnerability and exposure as I was?

The dictionary defines vulnerability as "being exposed to the possibility of being attacked or harmed, either physically or emotionally." So by definition, being vulnerable is dangerous. It's unsafe and unsettling. But if you choose to keep your gift under wraps and shield yourself from any possible humiliation, it leaves you with a deep void.

Here's what I know: you have a special gift inside of you—we all do—and if you aren't letting that gift shine, it will irk you to your innermost core as you remain chained to a steering wheel behind your financed BMW when your gift so desperately wants to burst out of you and make a difference in the world. You must share your gift. It takes massive courage to be vulnerable, but by vulnerably giving your gift away it fills you with incomparable joy, love and creative inspiration.

THEY ARE CALLED *GIFTS* FOR A REASON. THEY ARE MEANT TO BE GIVEN AWAY.

Steward Your Gift

Along with feelings of unworthiness and insecurity, the other great enemy to your gift is *busyness.*

I recently taught a room full of twenty-something women about nutrition, and I asked them to raise their hands if their lives were busy. Predictably, every hand shot up. Their faces told the all-too-well-known story: they were stressed and weary and they really just wanted me to finish the training so they could go home and convalesce before having to do it all over again the next day. It made me sad. I saw all the hidden treasures within these young, powerful ladies that weren't being stewarded due to being overwhelmed.

Everybody wants to make a difference. The problem is that most people are stressed out beyond belief from taking on way too many commitments that result in nonstop busyness. We are addicted to busy.

"How are you doing?"

"Busy."

"What's new?"

"I'm busy. Just so, so busy."

"Sorry to hear that. What does little Johnny want for his birthday tomorrow?"

"Oh! I've been so busy I haven't even thought that far ahead!"

"Well... we should catch up when you get time."

"Sorry, life is just so crazy-busy right now. I hope things will settle down soon."

Newsflash, my friend! Things will *never* settle down unless you choose to start living your life differently. When it comes to starting your business, there will never be a "good time", and your life will never become "less hectic." You need to put aside the excuses and get to work on what you were born to do.

Busyness does not automatically equal importance, productivity, or a meaningful life.

By discovering your gift and designing your life in such a way that allows you to be a great steward of it every day, you will be flooded with significance.

Give your gift away. Someone is praying for it.

> *Life is too short to hide who you are.*

Clarity of Calling

"What is my purpose in life?" is a common and oftentimes unsettling question. Many of us wander through life, confused and looking for clarity in finding our calling. I certainly didn't become clear until I was well into my 20s, an exploration that began when I hopped the pond for the very first time to study business in Milan.

I opted for the experience not because I wanted to eat gelato and drool over artwork for four months, but because I love a good challenge. It was a challenge to immerse myself in a foreign environment without knowing a soul upon arrival, public transportation that never ran on time, and no protein powder to be found. And, the only Italian I knew was, "Ciao!" Talk about challenging my comfort zone. It was just me, my suitcase full of spandex, a classic iPod with Timbaland's *Shock Value* on repeat, and an insatiable desire to grow up.

About halfway through the trip, my parents came to visit for my 21st birthday. Actually, my mom came to visit, and my Dad skittishly followed on a separate flight. Besides meeting in Milan, they had two separate trips altogether. My mom sipped wine in the south of France, and my dad toured around Italy taking pictures of the Leaning Tower of Pisa. All signs of awkward tension and lack of romance pointed to the "Big D" in the near future, although I wouldn't have admitted it then.

I spent much of my childhood worried about whether my parents would get a divorce or not. Many evenings were stolen by doors slamming and voices yelling, always with money seemingly the main instigator of dissatisfaction. The strong language and fierce tones hurt my spirit, so I would tuck away in my room and listen to music through headphones to drown out the chaos. We weren't poor, but things always felt tight. For a long time, my dad supported our entire family of seven single-handedly as a commercial realtor. When he made a sale, it was big, and it would carry us for a while. During those seasons of harvest, my parent's enjoyed themselves a lot more, and they would regularly make out in the kitchen. My youngest brother and I would complain—"Ewwwwww!"—but I secretly didn't mind. Seeing them kiss gave me a sense of security, like it was all going to be OK. However, as is the nature of real estate, things rarely happened in a timely manner, and in many cases, didn't happen at all. In seasons of drought, you could feel the stress and worry weighing on the shoulders of my parents.

I became very sensitive to money and the issues it could cause, and it was early on that I decided I would never begin a marriage under similar circumstances.

It wouldn't be until years later that I would realize my calling was deeply tied to my past.

———

When you find the intersection of purpose, passion, and utilizing your gift in your daily life, you are walking in the fullness of the purposes you were created for.

Purpose is the *why* behind a specific project.

Passion is the *what* to your *why*.

Your gift is the *how* to your *why*.

Calling is your life's *why*.

Your calling is the reason you were born. You aren't here by accident. You weren't dropped into your mother's belly at random. You aren't a mistake. You are chosen, and you are *called*.

Deep down, I always believed I was called to make an impact, but it wasn't until I asked myself one simple question that my life's calling became wildly obvious: *"What makes me mad?"* This question allowed me to approach my calling from a different angle, and now I see it as a mission I am uniquely designed to fight for.

I get **mad** when people lock up their dreams and say things like, "It could never happen for me."

I get **mad** when people stuff their God-given gifts deep down for nobody else to see.

I get **mad** when money tears families apart.

I get **mad** when people use time—or lack thereof—as an excuse for not creating what they are here to create.

I am called to empower people to fight through fear, use their gifts, and leave an impact. I'm here to awaken dreams. Through every conversation I have, every product I create, every song I sing, every word I write, and every message I give, I'm called to instill hope and truth.

Your calling is not a career.

It is not a project.

It is not a title.

It is not a hobby or passion.

Your calling is your life's work, and it is always tied back to helping others.

It also provides meaning to your past. You have been through trials, which have specifically tailored and equipped you to help others avoid those same things. The pain you have walked through is now your power.

When you are wrapped in your calling, you are the most YOU. You are in a joyous flow. You are on fire for life. And your energy is infectious. There's never been an easier time in the course of human history to begin fulfilling your life's mission than right now. Clarity of calling allows you to become unstoppable.

> *Life is too short to miss your calling.*

REFLECTION SECTION

These questions will help clarify your calling; how you will serve others.

- What makes you mad?
- What cause will being a Time Millionaire allow you to fight for?
- What pain do you want to help other people avoid?

Your Freedom Frees Others

True fulfillment during our short time on this planet comes from making an impact on the lives of others. But the sad truth is that most of us aren't even helping ourselves...

- 80 percent of Americans are in financial debt.
- 26 percent of adults have no savings set aside for emergencies.
- An estimated 38 million households in the United States live paycheck to paycheck.
- 40 percent of Americans are obese.
- The average US employee who receives paid vacation only takes about half of their allotted days.

The majority of people are stuck in a perpetual loop; they are living in survival mode, barely able to help themselves let alone able to help others. Just as they instruct on airplanes to put your oxygen mask on first, to be a Time Millionaire, you must understand that your freedom frees others. It starts with you—your purpose, your vision, your hustle.

Are you willing to serve?

If yes, you are on your way to a life of meaning and impact. I want to get you thinking about how you will serve with the abundant time you are going to have as a Time Millionaire. For starters, what would you do if you woke up to $100 million dollars in your bank account...if money were no object? Who would you spend quality time with? What projects would you contribute to? What would you create? Imagine for a moment: what would you do if you were no longer tied to your job, your debt, your commute, and all the stress associated with it? Your why is your boss. When you don't feel like showing up to that meeting, finishing a book, having a hard conversation, or taking the phone call, you need to remember why you started.

Fund your freedom with the ultimate side hustle so you can go out and free others.

> *Life is too short to live in survival mode.*

Now that you are clear on *why* it is urgent for you to become a Time Millionaire; so that you can impact the world with your gifts, pour into your passions and fully walk in the flow of your calling, it's time to get rooted in who you are and what you stand for to confidently pursue your dreams.

CHAPTER 2

CREATE CRAZY CONFIDENCE

Core Values

"Sunday, 6 p.m. Meet me on my magic carpet at Magnolia Park."

I first laid eyes on Sweet Jamesy on a hot summer night. It was a blind date. We had been text-flirting via Facebook, and he promised to only serve carrots and water if we met because he knew I was a fitness nut. By the time we had polished off the ahi tuna starter, bison kabobs, and the bottle of Maipo Valley Cabernet, I already knew he was my husband. It wasn't just his James Dean glossy eyes, his perfect white T-shirt that hugged his muscles, his relaxed diesel jeans, the fancy car he pulled up in, his ability to cook, or his impeccable attention to detail clearly demonstrated by this fairy-tale of a first date. I knew he was my soulmate because we just *got* each other.

Later on, as I dove further into personal development, I realized we "*got*" each other because we shared very key core values, such as creativity, authenticity, health, faith, personal growth, discovery, family, freedom, forgiveness, and integrity. Because our major core values were in alignment, I could easily picture us going through life together. Core values dictate your priorities. Core values help you make decisions quickly. Core values provide you with "balance."

People might say I live a very balanced life. I sleep 8-9 hours every night. I exercise six days per week. I continually fill our home with fresh groceries and spend loads of time with my husband. My business team and clients can always count on me, and I even have time to write a book. But it's not that I achieved perfect balance. It is simply that I sat down a few years ago and prioritized how I would prefer to allocate my time in accordance to my core values, and then I began to #HustleSmarter to create the reality. If you find yourself struggling with balance, what you are actually struggling with is priorities, determined by your core values.

WE DON'T HAVE A WORK-LIFE BALANCE ISSUE IN THIS NATION; WE HAVE A CORE-VALUES ISSUE.

Core values determine your decisions and behavior. Where you live, how much you spend, what you put your time and energy into—all affected by your values. People who are committed to their core values make decisions quickly and don't allow guilt to wrap up the opportunity cost of making a decision. They stand firm on their beliefs and work with their *why* in mind. Core values are your compass when decisions and opportunities arise.

By identifying and becoming rooted in your core values, it will boost your confidence when making decisions. You will no longer be a prisoner of indecision. Instead, you will be firm and take a stand for what matters most to you. This will give you immense freedom as you respond to the pressures of society, your family, etc. to do things a certain way. You must get clear on your core values and live by them to build your confidence as you work to become a Time Millionaire.

Chasing goals and dreams that are not congruent with your own deeper values is a recipe for disaster.

Life is too short to live out of alignment.

 REFLECTION SECTION

Identify your core values by writing a list of fundamental beliefs that guide your behavior and exemplify your priorities. This list can be as long as you need but generally the sweet spot is 5-10. One way to put your values to the test is to look at your bank account. What do you spend money on? For example, one of my core values is health. With multiple gym memberships, organic food box subscriptions, and a monthly budget for nutritional supplements, there is no doubt I value my wellbeing.

Self-Awareness

Becoming clear on your core values is the first step towards becoming self-aware, and self-awareness is key to improving your confidence. When you understand yourself better, you tend to act more consciously and be more compassionate towards yourself and others. In other words...you like yourself more! It is OK to like yourself, you know. In fact, being at peace with who you are will help you proactively manage your thoughts and emotions, thus improving your confidence to take on any dream written on your heart.

My interest in fitness began in elementary school when I stopped at nothing to earn the President's Fitness Award each year, but it really blossomed in college. I dove into every book and magazine I could get my hands on to learn how to make the most of my workouts, and, let's be honest, the quickest way to rock a bikini with ease. Soon enough, an idea popped into my head: "What if I became a personal trainer? I could get paid to work out with people!!!!" I started perusing online for job opportunities in the fitness realm, and I quickly applied at a huge big-box gym to sell memberships. I wasn't qualified as a trainer, so I figured I could work on my selling chops, cozy up with the training staff, and eventually become a trainer.

Within 10 minutes of interviewing with the sales manager, he looked at me and said, "You know what? It sounds to me like you should be a trainer." He called the fitness manager over, and after a few more minutes of chatting, I walked away with a pep in my step and a new job as a personal trainer in the most populated gym in all of Seattle.

As soon as I graduated college, I took the first step towards freedom and went private with my personal training. This got me excited for a few months because I quadrupled my income overnight as I was no longer giving away 90 percent of my profits to a corporate globo-gym. However, even with that quick increase, it didn't take long for me to notice the intensity of hours I would have to maintain in order to pay my bills. So I did what most successful trainers think about doing: I set my eyes on owning a gym.

By the time I was 23, a training buddy of mine had become my business partner, and we opened our very own waterfront gym. I was on top of the world. But the honeymoon phase didn't last long. On a Wednesday at 5:55 a.m. in early November 2010, just six short months after the grand opening, I walked up to the glass doors of the gym to open up shop only to find the locks had been changed. My business partner was sending me a (not so) subtle message that he was ready to part ways.

For several months we had been trying to hash out our differences. We hired a business coach for $1,000 an hour and had many sit-down discussions in the privacy of our massage room, but things were just getting messier. Our degree of wisdom was laughable at best. My maturity level wasn't even high enough to understand the importance of sharing core values with someone you go into business with. I walked away from my dream that day with my loyal clients by my side and an extra $25,000 of debt to boot. I was absolutely crushed. It took me nine long months to even begin feeling like my confident, futuristic self again, and it wasn't until I walked through full forgiveness of my ex-partner (and myself) that I was truly free to move on.

Although this was one of the darkest times of my life, the failure and loss catapulted me into a journey of self-discovery. For the first time ever, I stopped simply doing and started actually *being*. Being present. Being reflective. Being forgiving. Being thoughtful. Through mourning the loss of this dream, I started becoming truly aware of who I am and what I stand for. As hard as it was, I'm grateful for that season as it was necessary for me to get rooted in who I am.

Now that you are clear *why* you want to live a freedom-based lifestyle, it's time to become the person required to get it. The first steps toward true success are always inward. Successful entrepreneurs know how to master who they are and how to harness their inner power, instincts, and intuition. They are clear on what they value and how to act in alignment with their values. You must master your emotions, find freedom in discipline, and cultivate wisdom. Through this process, you will develop the confidence needed to march towards your destiny. Becoming self-aware now can save you from making an epically poor business decision like I did.

BEFORE YOU CREATE YOUR BUSINESS YOU MUST FIRST CREATE YOUR SELF.

The best thing leaders can do to improve their effectiveness is to become more aware of what motivates them and their decision making. What you're going to learn in the next few pages is what holds most people back from ever seeing their dreams realized. Even if they identify their purpose, do the goal setting, and then take action to get their business started—if they skip the inner work, the business will inevitably come tumbling down, one way or another.

You must establish a rock-solid foundation by having a staff meeting with yourself. Look in the mirror. What do you see? Do you see worthiness? A diamond in the rough? Or, are you showing up half-authentically? This journey will expose your weaknesses, but it will also skyrocket your strengths.

**IF YOU ARE CONSISTENTLY AND AUTHENTICALLY YOU,
YOU WILL NEVER REGRET IT.**

So, how do you become more...*you?* Below are three steps you can take to cultivate self-awareness.

1. **Keep a journal.** Self-reflect by physically writing down your thoughts, beliefs, and ideas to free your mind. Commit to a regular journaling practice and you will get a better idea of who you are and what is most important to you right now.
2. **Ask for feedback.** Allow your trusted friends to offer insight on their honest view of you. This will bring to attention possible areas in your life you can improve to be the best, truest you.

3. Practice self-discipline. I will be diving deeper into habits in the next section, but know that self-discipline helps you improve self-awareness by teaching you to control your desires and impulses in order to achieve a goal that is important to you.

To become a successful Time Millionaire, you must know thyself. Your best self is your solid foundation. You need to know your weaknesses, strengths, beliefs and desires. A strong sense of self will be the catalyst to grow your confidence and take your potential to an entirely new level. Knowing thyself will also make it more clear what habits you need to focus on in order to make a bigger impact.

> *Life is too short to build your legacy on sand instead of rock.*

 REFLECTION SECTION

If you haven't already, this is your friendly reminder to invest into a new journal to record your thoughts and dreams as a way to cultivate self-awareness...and house all of your answers to these reflection questions!

Creating Habits

"You can't get rich if you don't make your bed!" commanded an 80-something-year-old man from the front of the room during a Saturday conference on developing a 'Millionaire Mindset.'

I sat upright in my chair. I was 21 years old, and I don't believe I had ever made my bed willingly. He went on to describe the process of building wealth as the byproduct of developing exceptional habits. This was actually quite encouraging to me, because besides the state of disarray I generally left my home in, I was already in tune with developing great habits.

In high school, my parents never once asked if I had homework. I simply did it because I knew it needed to be done. They also didn't give me a curfew. I made sure I got plenty of rest to lead and perform well in class and in extracurricular activities. I put myself on an exercise schedule starting in the 9th grade to ensure my conditioning was exceptional for soccer tryouts. When other kids started getting into alcohol and drugs, I was never remotely interested, because I was too concerned with my performance and reputation.

Developing discipline is critical to your success. Success is about doing a lot of things you don't want to do so that you can ultimately reap the benefit of doing the things that matter to you most. It requires intentional change and sacrifice. As hard as it might be, if you want to live an extraordinary life, you must discipline your thoughts, words, and actions to be exemplary.

This wise old man, who would eventually become a huge mentor in my life, continued on: "Early in life, we choose our habits; later in life, our habits choose us."

I take daily inventory of my habits, although some seem harder than others to confront. Like overeating and drinking. While globetrotting with Jamesy for eight months on #GarnersGoGlobal, I was unapologetically gluttonous.

It all started with our two months in Italy where it is virtually a sin to order a beverage without complimenting it with something savory. We developed an afternoon negroni routine and were served with bottomless potato chips. Chips upon chips with one part gin, one part vermouth, and one part Campari garnished with an orange slice and served on the rocks in an old-fashioned glass.

And on and on continued these eight months of zealous eating. Nutella gelato in Rapallo that melted faster than I could lick. 9-hour slow-grilled rib eye and doughy empanadas paired with Malbec in Mendoza. Oven-fresh thick-crusted focaccia bread set perfectly with un caffe in Rome. Pho for breakfast in Vietnam. Succulent split-roasted lamb and the freshest oysters in the world, directly out of the water just minutes before, only needing a drip drop of lemon to slurp down in Croatia. And don't get me started on the Plavac grape, properly aged and fermented for my taste.

Like I said, gluttonous.

I never felt guilty, per se, but it certainly felt extreme at times. I recognized that anything is permissible, but that doesn't make it beneficial. Especially coming from a background in bodybuilding where one of your main job requirements is to try not to think about eating and to certainly not do it for sheer pleasure.

Upon our return, I was well aware my daily food and drink fest was going to need a complete overhaul if I wanted to lose the ten extra pounds I had come home with as well as model high leadership for my team. It was an integrity issue. First, James and I decided that we would not allow alcohol in our home. Any alcohol consumption would be at the occasional outing or gathering. This worked OK. Certainly better than when we were traveling, but it still wasn't enough. We were only three miles from over 140 wineries in Woodinville, Washington, and we quickly discovered a local neighborhood brewery that we grew accustomed to dropping by weekly for cold ones. The habit just adjusted to new environments.

By the fall of that year, I had become disgusted with my nonexistent results. Clearly, my haphazard efforts weren't getting me closer to my long-lost svelte self, so I decided to do something drastic: cut alcohol completely for an entire year. It seemed to be the instigator for bad food choices and excess calories, not to mention lackluster workouts and energy, so I cut it cold turkey. According to Gretchen Rubin, author of *Better Than Before: Mastering the Habits of Our Everyday Lives*, one of the best ways to create new habits is through what she calls a 'Blast Start'. Habits are the key to all of our successes and challenges in life, and changing habits with the Blast Start has worked wonders in my own life and in the lives of the people I coach.

The Blast Start is the opposite of taking the smallest possible first step because it requires a period of high commitment. It is going all-in on a goal. By definition, it is unsustainable over the long term, but it works extremely well at producing momentum.

This is the approach I use when coaching my clients on our nutrition jumpstart. The program pushes them to make their health an absolute priority for 80 days, and it produces incredible results. At the end of the 80 days, we are able to very smoothly transition into a manageable, healthy lifestyle for the long run.

Ultimately, whether you take small steps or go with a Blast Start, there's no right or wrong way to develop new habits. Do whatever works for you! The courageous choice to confront your habits and make a change has a ripple effect. It creates confidence to continue developing better habits. Everything feeds off each other.

People don't decide their future; they decide their habits.

Life is too short to be ruled by bad habits.

 REFLECTION SECTION

Write down either one good habit you are committed to developing or one negative habit you are committed to eliminating. Choosing not to do something is still choosing to do something, so it doesn't matter which way you look at it. Likely there are a handful of habits you could choose from, but I beg of you—just start with one! You will go big with your transformation by starting small. Everything big starts small.

Healthy Lifestyle

Choosing to live a healthy lifestyle is the entry point for discipline in your life. With the exception of a few rare cases, there is no excuse to ignore adherence to a regimented workout schedule. There is no excuse to fuel your body with junk the majority of the time. Regardless of your work schedule, life demands, budget or injuries, there is always a way to get out of your desk chair and move your body. There is always a way to get your hands on nutrient-dense food. It is simply a decision. And it is crucial to your success as an entrepreneur.

There are five major components that go into being your healthiest self: food, nutritional supplements, sleep, stress management, and physical activity. If any of these aspects are ignored, you are unable to perform at your best, resulting in a decrease of confidence. So, where do you stack up? Do you give yourself care in all five of these areas? Something I discovered as a personal trainer is that adhering to a regular workout routine is a big struggle for many.

Fitness is my jam. It was a passion birthed out of wanting to outperform my opponents on the soccer field and win pageants while I was at it. Part of the reason I work out is to strengthen my discipline and gain credibility with myself by showing up and putting in the work on something that offers me no intrinsic pleasure. Without fail, I run, lift, hit a CrossFit class, swim, practice yoga, perform barre, or do indoor cycling a minimum of five times per week. Much of the time, I am anything but jazzed to be hitting the gym, but I force the behavior regardless. My body, mind, and soul crave the clarity that comes with movement, and I feel the truest to who I am when I am disciplined with my fitness.

Confidence exudes when you make a lifelong commitment to be your healthiest self. This is the type of confidence where energy changes when you walk into the room. The type of confidence people are drawn to. The type of confidence that pushes you to march towards your dreams amidst adversity and discouragement.

You don't have to be a fitness model. You don't have to run marathons. You don't have to wear a size 4. But you do need to make your health a priority.

Here are four commitments I recommend you adhere to (at the bare minimum!):

1. **Sweat 4-6 times a week.** Run, lift, do yoga, spin, hike, dance. It doesn't matter how you do it. Just move that body! Any type of movement for 20 minutes minimum. Sitting is the new smoking and it needs to be combatted with regular physical activity. No excuses!

2. **Eat green vegetables every day.** There is so much I could cover on nutrition here, but I want this to be ridiculously simple. EAT YOUR GREENS! Spinach, kale, broccoli, brussels sprouts, green beans, asparagus, and/or arugula. Get them in at least once per day. No excuses!

3. **Discipline your sleep schedule.** Sleep deprivation is an epidemic. Nobody hustles smart on 5 hours of sleep! Do what it takes to schedule 8 hours of consistent sleep every night. No excuses!

4. **Take a daily probiotic.** Quality supplements fill nutritional gaps in your diet and can dramatically improve your energy, recovery, immunity, and gut health, as well as decrease

inflammation. There are a handful of hugely beneficial vitamins and supplements I could list here, but I believe the most necessary is a daily probiotic to aid in healthy digestion and boosting resistance to sickness. And no, yogurt alone will not allow you to reap the full benefit of these wonder bacteria.

Disclaimer: I am not a doctor and this belief is based on my own personal testimonial. Email me here: hello@angiegarner. com and I will show you how you can get your hands on the probiotic I have used and trusted for 10-plus years.

Bottom line: figure it out. Stop starting and stopping. Hire a coach. Go ALL-IN on creating healthy habits, one at a time. Refuse to let another day go by pushing your fitness goals under the rug.

> *Life is too short to be sick, tired, or*
> *lack the confidence needed to be successful.*

 REFLECTION SECTION

Do you abide by all four of these recommendations? If not, which of the four are you committed to implementing immediately?

Morning Routine

I am most certainly not immune to complacency. Sleeping in and snuggling with my husband, skipping a workout because of poor planning, and relaxing on the couch in lieu of making phone calls have all seduced me at times. However, I know complacency is a dream-stealer, so when I feel complacency slipping into my lifestyle, the first place I look to make an adjustment is my morning routine.

A morning routine sets the tone for your entire day, and it, in turn, sets the tone for your business and life.

The most important part of your morning routine is that you have one! Most people I talk to lie in bed as long as they can, and after pressing the snooze button four times, drag themselves from beneath the covers and jump right into a frantic day. Kids, coffee, dog, news, breakfast, traffic. Sound familiar? It is likely you will need to get up earlier to make a morning routine happen, but guess what? You can go to bed earlier! It's an easy fix. Stop with the late-night Netflix binges and social media addiction. Make your morning and sleep routine a priority and watch your world transform for the better.

Your morning routine is subject to your unique lifestyle and goals, but I wanted to offer a peek at what works for me to give you an idea of how I define a morning routine. Also, I highly recommend Hal Elrod's book *The Miracle Morning* to help you design and navigate the best routine for your specific lifestyle and goals.

Here are the five components of my 60-minute morning routine:

1. Hydrate and Caffeinate: 5 Minutes

Within minutes of my feet hitting the ground, I take my vitamins with a glass of cold water made alkaline with fresh-squeezed lemon juice. I then transition to a refreshing serving of Spark™ for the maximum mental focus to take on my day.

2. Movement: 10 Minutes

I roll out my yoga mat and do some very basic, light stretching to get my blood flow going. Childs pose, downward dog, bird-dog, and pigeon pose are a few of my go-to's. I also use this time on the mat to develop gratitude by meditating on all that I am thankful for.

3. Jesus: 30 Minutes

As a believer, I long for intimacy with Christ. During this segment of my morning, I read *The Voice Bible* and pray about my day ahead, as well as anything troubling me. I will also often do listening prayer by asking God for direction in a specific area and wait in stillness for his answer.

4. Visualization: 10 Minutes

Visualization is a crucial part of my routine. I allow myself to truly feel all the feels of what it will be like to reach the goals I am fighting for. I picture the successes I will have that day. I picture the woman I am becoming and the fruit that will come as a result. I think about my future children and the joy they will bring. I will expand more on this practice in Chapter 5.

5. Day Preparation: 5 Minutes

At this point in my routine, I am full of vigor and excitement for the day ahead. I open up my journal and write out my to-do list to keep myself accountable to my daily goals. Even things like groceries and workout go on this list because everything takes time. I generally tackle one business project per day on top of my regular commitments to my team and networking in the community.

Notice none of my routine includes scrolling newsfeeds. I use my phone as a timer but restrain myself from checking any social media, texts, or email before 8 a.m. I will even put it in airplane mode if I am tempted. This is to protect my thoughts and energy. It's so easy to go on a downward spiral of negativity in the news or comparing myself to the Instagram girl who is in Portofino. Again.

Does a 60-minute routine sound overwhelming? Not to worry. Just start somewhere. When I was working full time as a trainer and my first client was at 6 a.m., I had a 10-minute morning routine. I love, love, love the luxurious time I have now that I am a Time Millionaire. I can't wait for you to get here.

> *Life is too short to let your day run you instead of you running your day.*

Inner Circle

How you feel about yourself is also greatly impacted by the company you keep. If you surround yourself with friends who are self-aware and living intentionally, you are much likelier to be self-aware and intentional. With this in mind, I have always been highly discerning in regards to who I let in my inner circle. I have many acquaintances, but only a select few I spend ample time with. One of my dearest friends, Brynn (the "B" in D & B), offers an example of how the right influences can impact you for the better.

Brynn really doesn't miss a note with the dandiest of details. Her perfectly put together outfits, makeup, matching handbags and nails, music playlists, and menus, all of it premeditated. She is friendly, thoughtful, and genuine, and she makes everything pretty. Cats love her a lot too. She moves like a European, slow and methodical. She loves to take her sweet time and enjoy every moment in the present. She is also very generous, and she will give you the shirt off her back, which is almost undoubtedly from Anthropologie, so #winning. Probably the only thing that would cross her would be using garlic powder instead of fresh-minced. As you can imagine, because she is so attentive to detail, she isn't the timeliest of people. The running joke amongst our friends is to tell her we are meeting an hour before we actually plan to so we can ensure she makes it on time. And, please, by all means, do not show up to her dinner parties at the actual time she sets them. Be fashionably late. Always!

So, we are basically opposites. But that is not necessarily a bad thing. In fact, I continually learn how to be an improved human through her friendship.

She teaches me to savor life. She displays compassion for every living thing. She both encourages and challenges my ideas. She and Dan (the "D" in D & B) have similar goals and values as James and me, and those goals allow us to grow together and expand each other's thinking. They are our people. Who are your people?

We interpret our values and principles based on the people we surround ourselves with, which is why it is extremely important to be selective with your inner circle.

Isolation is the enemy to your destiny. We are created to be in a community. You cannot thrive alone. You need people who will support you and believe in you on your quest to become a Time Millionaire and pursue big dreams. A strong inner circle will inspire you with new ideas and motivation, providing accountability and a sense of belonging.

Don't surround yourself with just anyone. Instead, be super intentional about community and commit to relationships with on-purpose people. Science proves that we become like the people we associate with, so if you want to maximize happiness and lower stress, hang with people who embody the traits you desire. This is an actual strategy for living a more meaningful, impactful life! You can be the catalyst to start changing your environment by carefully choosing your inner circle.

Your friends determine the direction and quality of your life.

Life is too short to let the wrong friends tether you to mediocrity.

 REFLECTION SECTION

Think about those you are closest to. Are your friends living out their purpose? Giving themselves to something other than themselves? You will know because it's contagious. The joy is contagious. The drive is contagious. What can you do to surround yourself with more people in alignment with your values?

Finding a Mentor

Another way you can enhance your confidence and expand your inner circle is by aligning yourself with mentors who have already succeeded at a similar goal you are chasing. A great mentor will be that voice of positivity, reaffirming you that if they did it, you can do it too.

Every time I aim for a new goal in a new realm of expertise, I go on a search for someone who has already done what I want to accomplish. I have spiritual mentors, business mentors, marriage mentors, fitness mentors, and financial mentors. I have mentors who scare me, but I kind of like that. I have mentors who come and go depending on the season. I've paid mentors a lot of money, and I've had mentors who guide me out of their desire to simply make a dent on my life—or because I mentor them in a different area and it's a give-and-take.

There's a common idea that getting a mentor is about searching for someone who encompasses everything you want and then taking them to dinner and asking them to mentor you. That's one way to go about it, but I can't say I've ever done that. Mentors have more or less fallen into my lap as a result of me seeking change and transformation. If there is something I want to become excellent at—let's say public speaking— I won't hesitate to go out and find a group of like minds to network with. Every Tuesday at noon, I meet with my Toastmasters group, which is an organization with clubs around the world designed to help members improve their communication, public speaking, and leadership skills. A few of the seasoned members have become my mentors. They offer feedback, critique, and encouragement. They are continually raising the bar and challenging me. They tell me the truth, even when it hurts. That's what mentorship is for.

Don't overcomplicate mentorship, and don't ignore it. Whether you pay for it or not, you do need to follow in the footsteps of someone who has the fruit in their life you're after in that particular area. One of the most incredible things about network marketing is that mentorship is built into the business model. There is someone in your upline who has had success, and you simply need to plug into what they are doing and model their behavior. They will pour into you as long as you are coachable and producing results. You can both benefit, so it is a win-win.

This may seem obvious, but I have witnessed people take some pretty bad advice from unreliable sources so I must address it: make absolutely sure the person you are being coached by has the success you're after. Don't take financial advice from your broke 55-year-old uncle. Don't take health advice from your friend who is a chronic yo-yo dieter. Don't take business advice from someone who has never successfully run the type of business you're building. Be extremely careful who you let speak into your life. And, likewise, be extremely careful what you speak into other people's lives.

As you build your confidence, grow a business and become more influential, you will also begin to attract people who want to be mentored by you. Keep this in mind as you are learning from your own mentors. Be coachable. Be loyal. Be observant. Take your mentee role seriously, as every great leader is first a great follower.

REFLECTION SECTION

In your current season of life, which of these areas are you most seeking growth in: health, finances, business, marriage, or faith? Once you have chosen a specific area of focus, make a list of possible mentors, coaches or groups you could align with to learn from.

Ready or Not

Does the idea of mentoring other people scare you a little bit? If so, that's OK, and it is actually quite common. Perhaps you don't feel qualified, or you don't want to let anyone down. One of the best ways to overcome feelings of inadequacy is to jump in before you feel ready.

My junior year of high school I suddenly found myself wanting to become drum major of the high school marching band. This prompting came from dating the bandiest of band nerds. He made it look super cool and inspired me to do the same. There was only one problem: I had never been in band before.

The first step was to actually join the band. Developing an embouchure to play brass or woodwind was out of the question as I would be going up against seasoned musicians who had been playing since the 5th grade—so I opted for the drum line.

Keeping a rhythm isn't that hard, right? They put me on the bass drum. I figured it was a win-win as I got to play music and burn tremendous calories at the same time. I diligently pounded away without anybody knowing my top ambition to become the "big cheese." My boyfriend started teaching me drum major-y skills in the off-hours, as I knew tryouts would be at the end of the school year.

Tryouts came, and I was certainly the least qualified amongst my opponents, but I did have one advantage: many incredible musicians didn't even give it a go! I had a glimmer of hope. I put on my pageant smile and worked that baton. I conducted the national anthem with confidence, and when they announced my name as drum major at the end of the week over the loudspeaker, I was beyond myself. Football games would never be the same.

Often we exclude ourselves from our dreams because we listen to lies that tell us we are unqualified, unworthy, or unequipped. The thing is, you're going to fail 100% of the time if you don't try. If you do try, you're already reducing your chances of failing substantially. Don't kill your confidence by quitting before you even start. If you are in such a position, if you find yourself wanting more, if you feel you are playing small, if you feel you aren't ready to start and run a business, I promise, you are not alone. To overcome it and see the success you want, you must push those thoughts away enough to take the next step. And then the next step. And then the next step. Your confidence will grow little by little as you take action and walk into your calling. It's the only way. Nobody can do it for you. YOU have to step into uncertainty to grow.

**ONE STEP AT A TIME IS HOW YOU WALK OUT
YOUR DESTINY.**

It may be scary, but it's far scarier living a complacent life, hiding behind your insecurities.

> *Life is too short to not take the next step
> towards your dreams.*

 REFLECTION SECTION

Is there a dream you are currently procrastinating on because you don't feel qualified? If you were to start moving towards fulfilling that dream, what would be your immediate next step? It could be as simple as educating yourself in that area by picking up a book or signing up for a conference on that subject. Take action on that step TODAY.

Confidence Killers

In my younger years, I was teased heavily for believing in myself and my dreams. Many kids couldn't make much sense of it, so they categorized me as being "self-absorbed." I struggled with this label for a long time. How was I to be confident without being arrogant? Was it wrong to have faith in my potential? Perhaps some of the judgment was kids being kids, but what if there was truth to it? How could I show people I believed in them as well? Interesting thoughts for a 5th grader, I know.

Sometimes people shy from walking with confidence because they don't want to appear arrogant. But, to not believe in yourself is a surefire way to avoid an extraordinary life. There is actually a distinct difference between arrogance and confidence:

- Arrogance says, "I'm better than you."
- Confidence says, "I believe in me."

Everything you want in life is on the other side of confidence. You must believe your dreams were given to you for a reason and every skill required to see those dreams through are skills you already have or have the ability to develop. There are, however, confidence killers that have the ability to stop you in your tracks. Diligently work to avoid the following four confidence killers listed below on your journey to become a Time Millionaire.

1. Procrastination

Prolonging something hard only makes it harder. It wears at your self-esteem. It creates voices in your head telling you ridiculous notions, such as "You aren't good enough" and "You are unworthy." The longer you go, the more the self-doubt grows like a weed in your mind. Taking action is by far the most effective way to put those voices to rest and build your confidence. Sure, you may feel unprepared or ill-equipped, but you just have to do whatever it is that will move the ball down the field closer to your goal.

2. Comparison

Comparison leaves you feeling defeated and helpless, and if unattended to, it can leave you settling for misery. You have nothing to gain from it and everything to lose. As a highly competitive person, comparison has stolen more of my own joy than I wish to recall. Consistently counting your blessings and writing down what you are grateful for works wonders in pulling you out of a comparison trap.

3. Perfectionism

Being a perfectionist is having the aim to make others feel inferior. This goes hand-in-hand with arrogance, as we discussed earlier. Instead of striving for perfection, set your eyes on excellence. Excellence is doing the best you possibly can with the circumstances you are presented. It brings the best out of everyone around you.

4. Negative Self-Talk

What you speak out of your mouth is what comes from your heart. And if what comes from your heart is negative, your very words have the ability to breathe death into your dreams. You must get your words under control. Eliminate negative words and phrases, such as "never," "can't," "try," "should," "someday," "why me," and "I suck at." Stop claiming your defeat! Also, refuse to engage in gossip—it is poison. Change your words, change your life.

You cannot thrive as a Time Millionaire without confidence. You must believe in yourself! Confidence comes with knowing who you are, what you stand for, and what you are willing to fight for. Confidence comes by surrounding yourself with an encouraging and motivated inner circle. Confidence comes with action, and oftentimes that action must be taken in unfamiliar territories. Confidence comes with the development of exemplary habits. Commit to growing your self-confidence, and watch your business grow as a result.

> *Life is too short to talk yourself into living small.*

 ## REFLECTION SECTION

Which of these confidence killers do you most struggle with? What will you do to overcome it?

You are clear on what you want and why you want it. You are taking active steps to build your confidence and become the person to get it. Now, let's get into the mindset required to be a successful Time Millionaire.

CHAPTER 3

_____

MASTER YOUR MINDSET

Mo Money, Mo Problems?

We need it for food, shelter, and water. We want it for experiences
and blessing others. Money frees you up to contribute abundantly
with your time and resources. With money, you can do what you
want, when you want, how you want, and with whom you want.

"But Angie, what about all the happy poor people in
Africa?"

I didn't say money would make you happier, but it certainly
does give you more options. Money is a tool, and tools are meant
to be used. You can use this tool for good things, such as blessing
your friends and family with a vacation home on the beach they
can use to gather and retreat with no added financial burden. You
can also use this tool for bad things, like squandering your life away
smoking cigarettes and gambling at the casino. How you use money

will magnify what's really in your heart. It makes you more of who you already are. It also buys things like electricity and groceries. Useful, right?

"But Angie, what if the Notorious B.I.G. was spitting truth when he rapped, 'Mo Money, Mo Problems'?" I hear you, and I offer this #truthbomb in response: whether you have money or not, you will have problems.

When you don't have money, you have problems such as severely limiting time out with friends, driving an unreliable car that always seems to end up in the shop costing more money, and spending far too much time looking for deals and clipping coupons. Often, you can't see your family as much as you'd like because they are in another state and flying is not only expensive but requires more time off of work. Whenever a birthday or wedding comes up, you cringe as you start counting how much it will cost to even participate. You may just have to miss it this time. When you don't have money, you keep crawling back to your parents asking for money. If they even have money. When you don't have money and are raising kids, you become far too familiar with the word no and the look of disappointment on your children's faces. Financial problems are one of the leading causes of divorce, and why wouldn't they be? When you have two people fighting to survive with very little energy left over to connect and experience the beauty of life beyond kicking back on the couch every night in front of a TV screen, closeness wanes as credit card debt piles.

In my experience, you actually think about money a lot more when you don't have it.

When you do have money, you have problems such as people asking you for money more often, so you have to choose who and when and how much to give. You undoubtedly have a higher tax bill, but you also have more disposable income so taxes are not an actual problem if you plan accordingly. You have to constantly check your heart and decide if an increase in lifestyle is really worth the investment, or if your money is better spent impacting someone's life. These problems are related to the elevated level of responsibility that comes with mo' money.

And the best problem with having mo' money is you have to choose what to do with your time. Are you going to spend your days golfing and sailing into the sunset? Or are you going to unlock your gifts and continue to explore, create, connect, and contribute? With the occasional #yachtlife worked in too, of course. Cause #YOLO.

YOUR BELIEFS ABOUT MONEY CAN DRAMATICALLY HOLD YOU BACK FROM AN INCREASE IN YOUR LIFE AND BUSINESS.

Recently, I was sitting in a conference room with a handful of high-achieving career women and the subject of health insurance was brought up. One of the ladies was sharing her plight of getting smacked with a $3,000 medical bill right before the holidays, but as soon as the story left her mouth, she apologized. "I'm sorry—I know talking about money is poor form." *How sad!* I thought to myself. Money is something that needs to get talked about, and so many people are raised believing it is a naughty conversation topic.

Your past is not an excuse but it *may* be a reason you aren't moving forward. Perhaps belief systems were downloaded into you early on, and you heard things like, "Don't be silly, we can't afford that!" or "Trips to Hawaii are for the rich kids, OK?" or "Money doesn't grow on trees!" or even worse, "Honey, we have to move ... again." So instead of seeing money like the limitless tool it is, you've been taught to hold on to every last bit. SAVE, SAVE, SAVE, and then maybe you'll have enough to take that dream vacation and retire? Just maybe?

If your money mindset is off, you will not be able to achieve the levels you want financially and will certainly not be able to become a Time Millionaire. Free yourself from any negative feelings about money by acknowledging that money is simply a tool, and it is widely available to anyone who is willing to go out and get it. Money is also a reasonably accurate indicator of your value. So if you're struggling with money, focus on adding more value.

> *Life is too short to be broke.*

 REFLECTION SECTION

Do you feel your money mindset could be limiting you? What stories about money tend to replay in your head and how can you re-write them?

Ideal Income

There's a big difference between baseline income and ideal income. I can live off $10,000 per month, but I prefer to live off $100,000 per month. I could continue to pay thousands of dollars towards debt, but I prefer to live in complete freedom of debt. James and I could share a car or ride the bus, but we prefer to drive our own reliable vehicles. I'm a big fan of German-made. He likes Italian. Who knows, maybe the leather seats and horsepower won't be so exciting down the road and we will buy a mini van. Or not. What I do know is the vast majority of epic experiences in my life have required some serious dough.

Traveling around the world? Fundage. Dream wedding? Benjamins. Trips to visit family? Scratch. Business investments? Mula. Education? Dolla dolla bills, ya'll. Kids? I'll get back with you, but I heard they ain't cheap.

Also, there are all the not so fun things we need money for too. Like accidents and unplanned medical needs. New brakes for the car. Emergency vet visits. Bridge tolls. Data plans. But the most important thing money gives us? TIME.

**WHEN YOU HAVE MONEY WORKING FOR YOU,
IT FREES YOU UP IN A BIG WAY TO SPEND TIME
ON WHAT MATTERS MOST.**

James and I are working to increase our income beyond a million dollars per year to fund all the dreams written on our hearts. To take care of my parents as they age. To build the forever home I've been thinking about since I was a little girl. To give our children a real-world education where we take a weekend getaway to Boston when they are studying the founding fathers, we hop on a plane to Normandy to learn about World War II, we take a few weeks to explore India to learn about cultural differences, and we walk in the footsteps of Jesus by touring Israel. To continue funding creative projects, such as writing books and making videos. To bless our community and organizations we believe in. And so many more things we don't even know about yet.

> *Life is too short to just cross your fingers*
> *and hope everything works out.*

 REFLECTION SECTION

How much money will it take for you, on an annual basis, to chase your dreams, give back, and live in freedom?

- Here are typical expenses to consider:
- Rent or mortgage
- Automobiles (payment, insurance, gas, tolls, etc.)

- Health insurance
- Food (groceries, restaurants, etc.)
- Hobbies (music, sports, games, etc.)
- Gifts
- Donations
- Health and fitness (classes, trainer, supplements, equipment, clothing, etc.)
- Travel
- Business investments
- Clothing and toiletries
- Debt (student loans, cars, credit cards, business, taxes, etc.)
- Beauty (makeup, haircuts, nails, etc.)

What's your magic number? What does your lifestyle— or the lifestyle you want—require? Write it down.

Now, how much are you currently earning at your job/business/investments on an annual basis? Write it down.

Are the two numbers different? If so, we have some work to do. At least now you have a bull's-eye in mind.

Stop Being a Wussy

I'll never forget when I decided to stop being such a wimp about money. I invested $800 big ones into nutritional supplements, positioning myself to earn the highest amount of income possible with my hobby direct sales business. My credit card already had a stagnant balance of a few grand on it from a Nordstrom anniversary sale two years prior, so what was another $800? Still, it was scary for a recent college grad.

As time would tell, the further I stretched myself to take calculated risks, the faster my business grew.

By 2012, I had fully decided to pour my energy into building this direct sales business, and that year I earned just over $69,000 of 1099 income with my part-time efforts. Every penny of that extra income went to debt, taxes, and reinvesting back into my business. I didn't run out and buy a Range Rover or upgrade to a corner unit with a view. I stayed put, maintained my lifestyle, and poured money back into my team, travel, events, samples, an accountant, and so on. That discipline set me up to earn over $168,000 in 2013, paving the way for my freedom-based lifestyle at 26 years old.

Jamesy has a few plants around the house he tends to. He makes sure they get ample sunlight and the correct amount of water. He even speaks encouraging words over them. Weird, I know, but that's how I feel about investing into my business. I find great joy in it. I am like a farmer, tending to the seeds I have planted, giving them love and attention. I want to make more money to invest more back into my business so it has the fuel to grow even faster and bigger. This book? I paid for it myself. I paid for the editor, the conference I went to in order to learn how to write an outline, the cover design, the photo shoot, the PR, and even a coach to help me market it. I don't do GoFundMe campaigns for my business. I think that's great if it feels authentic to you, it just doesn't for me. I live in America where opportunity abounds. I know I can always hit the pavement and earn it with the right mindset and effort.

If you are a tightwad, you aren't going to do well with the #HustleSmarter lifestyle. Entrepreneurs fail when they aren't willing to spend money on marketing, events, systems, or their people. Investing into your business is about taking ownership. If you want to stay put in your J-O-B then the best way to do it is by being a wussy about money. Thankfully, beliefs can be changed when they no longer serve us or enable us to achieve our goals. If you have been a wussy, there is hope for you, just like there was for me.

Successful people understand they must invest both time and money to grow a business, produce more income, and reach goals. Not throwing money around foolishly, but wisely choosing strategic areas to invest back into an organization, a team, and/or an idea.

> *Life is too short to be a wimp about money.*

Time > Money

I don't know about you, but my to-do list often looks something like this:

- Call Comcast
- Order books
- Send birthday card
- Get groceries
- Cook dinner
- Respond to emails
- Follow up with product users
- Follow up with business builders
- Clean house
- Record podcast episode
- Write content for the blog
- Update the website
- Schedule a nail appointment
- Email my bookkeeper

...IT NEVER ENDS!

And these are the to-dos *on top of* my regular appointments, conference calls, daily workouts, laundry, and so on and so on.

And all that *on top of* my very most important roles: spending time with God and with Sweet Jamesy. I don't even have kids yet! Aye aye aye.

There's no way I can make traction on my business if I attempt to do everything as Wonder Woman super-wife. And neither can you.

Toilets are not my forte. Paying a housecleaner easily adds 3 hours back to my discretionary time and keeps our home sparkling for my OCD husband. Happy husband = happy life.

Here are some other services I regularly invest in:

- **Ongoing education ($5,000+ per year):** The more education I can absorb, the faster I can rock and roll. Courses and seminars and books are *packed* with the most important things to know about moving your business forward. If the topic is related to my current project, I don't think twice about investing.

- **Fitness classes ($400 per month):** I can discipline myself to work out on my own, but don't we all love a good push? I thoroughly enjoy the accountability and community of group classes.

- **Bookkeeping ($150 per month):** I would die without a bookkeeper and accountant. Taxes increase my heart rate. This is a very small price to pay to remain alive.

"But Angie, I don't have moneeeeey for all that!"

I didn't either. I started with the basics and went from there. Take one thing at a time. I'm not encouraging you to get into debt over these things, but certainly there is room for $20 a month to start an email list and grow your reach without having a big disorganized mess of contacts. Or $200 a month for a weekly babysitter so you can have meetings at your home with fewer distractions. Or $500 per year to have a qualified accountant file your taxes.

TIME IS YOUR MOST IMPORTANT ASSET.

Life is too short to be owned by tasks that aren't your highest and best use.

 REFLECTION SECTION

What investment can you make to free your bandwidth and put more of your energy towards the projects and tasks you are gifted at? Sign up for a meal delivery service? Hire a part-time nanny? A virtual assistant, perhaps? Or how about a personal trainer?

Fall in Love with Sales

In addition to overcoming any money blocks, in order to earn your freedom-based lifestyle you must have a healthy mindset when it comes to sales. If you have a negative opinion of sales, it is likely you felt pressured into buying something you didn't actually want at some point in your life, and it left you with a bad taste in your mouth. From that point forward, you decided sales was a dirty word and certainly wasn't anything you wanted to be associated with.

This thinking will kill your dreams of becoming a Time Millionaire. You must make a mindset shift and embrace the art of sales. As you will see, sales is actually a huge benefit for all parties involved if done with class and integrity.

I was no dummy growing up. I went to mom for the Nordstrom runs and to dad for the big-ticket items, such as computers and guitars. So, naturally, when I was 15.89 years old and it was time to make my play for a car, I pulled up a bowl of ice cream with Dad for a heart-to-heart.

My case went something like this, "Hey dadio, I'm going to apply for running start, which means I need to have transportation to both the community college and to the high school. Now I know you don't want to be my chauffeur driving across town [an average of 40 miles per day!], and I know you sure wouldn't mind me getting college credits while in high school. This investment will actually save you money. Not to mention I am involved in varsity soccer, dance team, the young republicans club, Earth club, leadership, pageants, track, and marching band. Why would you want to rob me of the joy brought by these resume-building activities because I can no longer bum rides off other parents? I need this for my future success. I'm on track to be a CEO of a mega-company. I would gladly contribute to the purchase, gas, and insurance, however, due to my immense involvement in bettering myself, there is no room for straight A's, extracurriculars, *and* a job. Also, due to weather conditions where we live, the car ought to be newer and safe [i.e., not a beater]. Plus, the three older kids all got cars when they turned 16..."

This was my first major sale.

I got my car, Subi (a 1998 Subaru Legacy), and somehow I also convinced my dad to spend about four times the amount he paid for all my older sibling's cars. I wasn't mad about it. My mom on the other hand...

You see, everyone sells. Just because you don't have the word "sales" in your job title does not mean you don't sell. You do. To your boss, to your partner, and to your friends. You sell the movie you want to see. You sell the new album you just downloaded. You sell the restaurant you want to try. You sell your ideas, your vision, and your favorite type of workout. You sell your employees on how great their job is. You sell yourself in interviews and on Tinder.

It is time that sales stops being a dirty word and is honored for what it is: an art form and a benefit to mankind. Matching needs and wants with products and services.

**SALES IS SIMPLY PROVIDING A SOLUTION
TO SOMEONE'S GOALS.**

You are a solution for somebody. So own it! There's a common thought that some people are just born "natural salespeople" and some people are not. I adamantly disagree. Sales can be taught and learned by anyone willing.

Here is an incredibly basic breakdown of how to make a sale:

1. Qualify and gain interest from a prospect looking for results in an area you offer a solution for.
2. Connect with this prospect by asking questions and getting to the root of why they want the outcome they're after.
3. Offer your product or service as the solution to this prospect's unique pain points.
4. Problem solve if any objections arise and make the sale.

DU*@0WOY^&*(#9839JJIA)_{(OD)_S!!!!!!!!!!

That was me getting excited because it REALLY IS THAT SIMPLE!!!

Sales also allows you to compress time. James and I are perpetually self-employed, so sometimes we joke, "Well, honey, if all hell breaks loose and for some reason our systems crumble, we always know sales." Meaning that if you know how to sell, you'll never go hungry.

If you love helping people, sales is for you.

"You will get all you want in life if you help enough other people get what they want."

Mindset shifts hurt. But if you've been carrying the preconceived notion that sales requires you to be pushy or annoying, you need to make a shift in your thinking. Fall in love with sales.

REMEMBER, YOU ARE A SOLUTION FOR SOMEBODY.

> *Life is too short to let your pre-existing ideas about something keep you from success.*

Taking Risks

One evening, I sat James down and told him we needed to talk. This was not unlike the time we convened three years prior to discuss our potentially controversial desire to elope. James was eager to hear what I had to say. I began explaining that it just didn't make a whole lot of sense to stay in Seattle longer than we had to. We had already booked our flights from Seattle to Peru to kick off #GarnersGoGlobal, our five-month trip around the world, for August 1st. It was now February, and our apartment lease was up April 30th. That left a three-month gap of either paying $3,200 per month to rent our uninspiring city flat month-to-month, find a short-term rental elsewhere (which would require us to move all of our stuff twice), or simply leave for our trip early.

Oddly enough, the idea came from my massage therapist.

As he was working a creak out of my neck, I was grumbling to him about the steep rent prices and my lack of interest staying in the construction zone of Seattle, and he matter-of-factly said, "Why don't you leave early?" Why of course. How silly of me to not seriously consider that. I suppose the idea of leaving for even five months stretched my level of discomfort further than it's ever gone, so adding another three months was never even on my radar.

I let dream-mode take over. I started researching Airbnb's in Italy. I've found that when you entertain just a glimpse of an idea, it often grows into something much bigger, stealing all of your thoughts in a good way. Before I knew it, I had devised the perfect two months in my favorite country: Milan to Lake Como to Florence to Tuscany to Liguria. We would return home for a few weeks in July to attend Success School, our national convention, and then we would continue on to South America.

I trusted the risk would be worth it, and naturally, our time in Italy was one of our favorite parts of the entire world trip. We couldn't even believe it wasn't a part of the original plan!

Risk makes you feel alive. It allows for otherwise unforeseen opportunities to emerge. It builds your confidence. It teaches you lessons. It helps you overcome a fear of failure.

To become a Time Millionaire, you must embrace risk. Taking a leap by committing to your business is a risk. But success won't just fall in your lap. You must pursue it. You must take the risk because of the freedom and joy that comes as a result.

THE *REAL* RISK IS NOT FOLLOWING THE DREAMS WRITTEN ON YOUR HEART.

Life is too short to risk not taking a risk.

 REFLECTION SECTION

Write down something you've always wanted to do but pushed the idea aside because you deemed it too risky. Seriously consider what you could do to move towards this dream. If it doesn't work, what's the worst that could happen?

Facing Fear

Risk is closely tied to its cousin: fear. Both involve putting your perceived safety on the line, oftentimes in the form of your ego being threatened. Facing fear is challenging, no doubt, but entrepreneurs have to face fear on a regular basis if they want to go far.

When I was a little girl, I watched *E.T. the Extra-Terrestrial* and suffered nightmarish consequences at bedtime. On nights when it was really bad, my mom would kneel down, lay her hands on me, and start changing the atmosphere with her prayers. She taught me how to command out thoughts and beliefs that weren't serving me. She taught me how to discern. She taught me how to seek God for comfort and clarity. She taught me how to rest in His promises.

I'm not scared of fake aliens anymore, but I do get nervous about failing when I take risks and try new things.

When I feel fear creep in, trying to attack from every angle, I do exactly what my mom taught me: I command the disbelief out. I discern that there are forces that don't want me to succeed, but I won't let them stop me. I press into the vision for my life and choose faith over fear. And then, I make a list.

Every time I'm on the verge of doing something scary, something that could possibly cause me to lose money, time, or make me look like a fool, I write out all the worst possible things that could happen. For instance, when we were about to start dropping serious coin on booking #GarnersGoGlobal, and I felt that surge of uncertainty rush through my belly, I made a list that looked something like this:

Worst Case Scenarios:

- I lose absolutely all momentum in my business and have to completely rebuild a six-figure income stream from the ground up.
- My team gets mad at me and stops trusting me, my friends don't like me anymore, and my mentors think I'm lazy and unfocused.
- James loses the last few deals he has in the pipeline, which could amount to over $100,000 in income.
- I leave my car in storage and mice build a home in the engine (I actually didn't think of this beforehand, but it did happen).

- We overspend entirely and come home broke.

- We can't find a suitable home when we return.

- Spiders infest our boxes in storage (I actually did think of this beforehand, and it really did happen).

- We run out of Spark™ (also happened and was also highly unpleasant).

- I get the Zika virus and don't even realize it until our first baby comes out with a smaller-than-normal head.

- We die in a plane crash.

- My laptop gets stolen.

After writing out these horrifying scenarios, it gave me a lot of peace knowing that, no matter what, I could survive most of them. It was going to be OK. My heart would still be beating. Unless there was a plane crash or terrorist attack. But that could also happen in the States, so really not an added risk.

FEAR IS SIMPLY THE ANTICIPATION OF PAIN. HOW DO YOU OVERCOME IT? YOU ACT IN SPITE OF IT.

It was our last day in Europe on our world trip. By the afternoon, I would be in the first-class Turkish Airlines lounge sipping on a glass of Öküzgözü while gearing up to depart for Thailand.

I was already feeling nostalgic. I'm a sucker for Europe, and I always will be. I feel at home with the rocky swimming holes, the fanciful old buildings, neighborhoods filled with the aroma of bread, and entire shops dedicated to cured meat and cheese that would make even a vegan cry tears of happiness.

To bid adieu to the beloved continent, I decided to open-water swim to and from a sunning spot at our cliff-side hotel in Dubrovnik, Croatia, out to a cave about a half a mile away.

The way there was just perfect. It was a refreshing workout, and resting on the hot pebbles in the sun-drenched cave felt well-earned and heavenly. After 15 minutes or so of basking in the October glow, I geared up for the return swim. Within a matter of minutes of being back in the choppy, deep blue waters, I felt a wave of something heavy come over me: fear.

All of a sudden, with no compelling reason besides our taxi driver told us there was a sighting in these exact waters a decade prior, I began imagining what I would do if I came face-to-face with a shark. The fear was instantaneous, and I couldn't stop visualizing the possibility. It stole all my joy in that moment and completely shifted my energy.

I stayed the course and did not end up as shark lunch, but it did get me thinking about fear. About how quickly it can start dominating your thinking. How suddenly it can consume your thoughts and steal your vision. How mischievously it causes you to question your ambitions and prevent you from taking action.

Making the courageous decision to continually challenge your comfort zone and fight through fear is the best thing you could possibly do for yourself on your path to success and significance as a Time Millionaire.

> *Life is too short to let fear dominate your thoughts and actions.*

 REFLECTION SECTION

What fear(s) are currently keeping you from moving forward? Action is the antidote to fear. Do something TODAY to fight this fear and boost your confidence.

Control Freak

One of the most common fears people have is that of losing control. Stemmed from perfectionism, the fear of losing control can have a crippling effect on your life resulting in excessive stress and anxiety. This is no way to live, and certainly not a strong mindset in which to build a thriving business upon. I trained myself early on to relinquish the grip of control in my own life is by surrendering to anything out of my control, and doubling down my efforts on the things I could.

I used to compete in pageants. I got to wear incredible amounts of rhinestones, meet world-changing women, and pay for college with the scholarship money I earned. Let's just say my back comb skills are on fleek. God bless Miss America.

There are five components of competition: talent, private interview, on-stage question, evening gown, and swimsuit. The winners are determined by a panel of judges. These are people with opinions and affinities for different things, and there is also the inevitable politics that come with a bunch of women duking it out. There are judging guidelines, of course, but I knew the outcome was never fully under my control.

I couldn't control whether the judges liked me, if I tripped in my stilettos, or hit a wrong note on the piano. I couldn't control the bad sound guys, butt-glue malfunctions, the pedigrees of the ladies I was competing against, or if anyone was going to show up to cheer me on.

What *was* in my control was the work I did on myself leading up to the event.

I could control the amount of practice and creativity I put into my talent piece.

I could control the discipline I put in at the gym and in my kitchen to strut across the stage in a swimsuit with confidence. And the tan. I could pay for that, at least.

I could control the reading and self-reflection I did to prepare for the interview.

I could control the gown I wore and the alterations to make it fit just right.

And this is what I chose to focus on. This is why I kept going back for more even after coming up short of a title time after time.

Life gets very messy and stressful when you put your thoughts and energy into things you can't control. That's why goals like "lose ten pounds" are unproductive. You can't control the scale! You can't control your body type or genetics. What you can control is what you put in your mouth, the physical activity you commit to, the community you surround yourself with.

I couldn't control getting turned down for every scholarship I applied for, or getting rejected from my top college picks despite my 3.97 grade point average and overwhelming resume of achievements. So I problem-solved. I drove to running start in high school to earn college credits and competed in pageants to ease the financial burden. I didn't have anxiety about it because I focused on what I could control.

You can control your routine. You can control showing up. You can control how you communicate and how you talk to yourself. You can control your attitude and your perspective. You can control what you read and what you listen to.

SUCCESS IS NOT A MYSTERY. IT IS A DAILY FOCUS ON IMPROVING WHAT YOU CAN CONTROL.

Life is too short to let the illusion of control be the thing that controls you.

 REFLECTION SECTION

Is the illusion of control keeping you from peace in your life right now? How can you release and surrender to walk into the flow of your calling with more ease?

You're So Lucky

"YOU'RE SO LUCKY!!! I'm so jealous. I wish I could do that."

I hear this phrase like a broken record when I share stories of our #GarnersGoGlobal adventure. Those exact twelve words, in that exact order. I've caught myself doing it too.

"She's so lucky she was born with that body type."

"They're so lucky their parents gave them money for a down payment."

"She's so lucky she grew up on the beach."

"She's so lucky she caught a big break and is an Instagram celeb and stuff."

This is an incredibly dangerous headspace to be in. If you genuinely believe people have fruit in their lives because of sheer luck, it completely disempowers you and takes hustle out of the equation. It enables you to live as a victim, feeling sorry for yourself, which will steal your dreams faster than just about anything else. Little to no action is taken, and you get lost in a funk of sadness and self-pity. On the contrary, if you wholeheartedly believe you are given the freedom of choice, it fuels your perseverance and drive. It helps you become a problem solver and an optimist, attracting opportunity and success.

Here are three steps you can take to break free from a victim mindset:

1. Take radical responsibility for everything.

Don't like the numbers in your bank account? Stop blaming the economy and get to work on your side-hustle.

Don't like the way you look in that group photo? Stop blaming your busy schedule and get yo' booty to the gym.

Don't like your unappreciative boss? Stop blaming her for your stress and make a job change.

Don't like how expensive your town is? Stop blaming corporate behemoths for taking over and just move already. Or increase your income.

Don't like the marriage prospects in your area? Stop blaming where you live and start saying yes to any opportunity to meet new people.

Don't like it when people ignore you? Stop blaming them for not returning your calls and start calling so many people it doesn't even matter.

Stop saying you're stuck. Stop complaining. Stop whining. Start owning the fact that you live in a country with the freedom of choice.

2. Develop a gratitude practice.

Gratefulness vaccinates you against the disease of entitlement. When you start and end each day reflecting on what you are grateful for, seeds of bitterness cannot take root. Instead of feeling that you never have enough—or never are enough—you begin to operate from a place of abundance, therefore attracting more into your life. When disappointing things happen, train yourself to ask, "What can I learn from this experience?" Even difficult outcomes can result in thankfulness if your mindset is strong.

3. Find freedom through limitless forgiveness.

In March of 2015, I was at the gym lifting weights at 7 a.m.-ish, and as soon as I had warmed up and was going to rep out some squats, I felt a holy promoting to go to a specific waterfront park. Say what?! I battled the idea. Because, traffic...and leg day. But it felt overwhelmingly clear.

I hopped in my MINI and headed down the hill. As soon as I parked, there was a mist over the lake, and I felt my next instructions were to roll out my yoga mat on this bank. I instantaneously fell to my knees. At that moment, unforgiveness I had been harboring was revealed to me. It had been weighing me down for so long and was creating a massive roadblock. I forgave. I surrendered. I was changed. Everything changed.

Forgiveness sets you free. It is not about letting the other person off the hook—it is about you letting go of painful feelings. By surrendering resentment it makes room for emotional healing, and as an emotionally strong person who harbors no animosity, you cannot blame others.

I am fortunate to have James by my side to help me keep my mindset in-check. Recently, the winter rain slowed down and the nights started getting longer...time to dust off the grill! I bought a new tank of propane to prepare for a cookout and one day later when I went outside to fire it up, the tank was gone! Someone had stolen it overnight. I felt a bit violated and was both equally angry that I had to make another trip to the store for a new tank, and I couldn't make us burgers that night. It's so easy to fall into a victim mentality when unfortunate things like this occur, but the moment

I began to complain, James gently stopped me in my tracks, "Well, we should have put a cover on our grill." Radical responsibility. He kept me accountable to the right mindset and I quickly responded, "You're right. And thank goodness we have $50 to buy another one." Gratitude. I concluded that whomever stole the tank must have been pretty hard up to do such a thing. I let it go. Forgiveness.

You have the power to change your circumstances through your choices. Let go of any victimhood so you can be free and make an impact as a Time Millionaire.

> *Life is too short to fall prey to a victim mentality.*

Your purpose is unfolding. Your confidence is growing. Your mindset is shifting. Now, let's get into the what of the ultimate side hustle and get detailed on how it will bring you freedom.

CHAPTER 4

THE ULTIMATE SIDE HUSTLE

The Silver Bullet

"No way will I *ever* be one of *those* people!"

I fought it kicking and screaming. I thought I was above it. That I was too creative. Too entrepreneurial. I had convinced myself people who were in those types of businesses were desperate.

And yet, so was I.

I was desperate for freedom. I had always imagined a completely different life than what was playing on my personal movie reel. With my 25th birthday around the corner, I had no viable way to get ahead financially except through the protein powder in my cupboard. Finally, I shed my ego, kissed my pride goodbye, and opened myself up to what was possible.

There is no such thing as a "silver bullet." But networking marketing is the closest you'll come to one.

It is a business in a box. It is ready-to-go...all it needs is your voice, your ability to connect, and your grit and determination. You don't have to worry about product design or legal headaches or ten-page business plans. You don't need business partners. You don't have to hire a coach to learn the ropes. You don't need a certification or a four-year degree. You don't have to hire employees or deal with the overhead of a storefront. The startup cost is pennies in comparison to any other entrepreneurial adventure. The products, the compensation plan, the mentorship—it's all there waiting for you to say yes. Not to mention that you can turn a profit on day one of opening your business.

I was a product user for three years before I made the decision to go all-in on the opportunity. When I was at my breaking point and knew something had to change if I ever wanted to spend quality time doing the things I love with the people I love, I made a list of every single option I could pursue to make more money and to eventually leverage my time. There were ideas for websites and apps and online training programs. I even wrote down the possibility of (*gasp*) getting an actual job. But, that would require commuting in Seattle traffic, and it certainly wouldn't allow me to wear spandex every day, so I ruled it out quickly. What pushed me over the edge to land on direct selling was the clear evidence for potential success. I knew, without a doubt, I would get out of it what I put into it.

Also, I was broke. I didn't have the ability to fund any other idea on my own without going further into debt, and the thought of searching for funding sounded downright exhausting. I still owed $25,000 to a few generous clients who supported my vision of opening a gym. And even if I got another business idea funded, there was no guarantee I would earn the type of income I was after, let alone any guarantee that I would even turn a profit. I knew it in my gut: I was called to this company and to network marketing, and it was time to embrace it.

One thing I am not going to do is pretend like everything is sparkly rainbows and kumbaya around the campfire at every gathering once you sign up. You are running a real business, with real challenges, working with real people.

So let's get real: I never truly understood patience until I started my business. There are times I want to throw my phone across the living room. Pray for me. Please. There are people who are more comfortable playing victim than stepping into their greatness. There are people more addicted to their excuses than their dreams. You will witness so many people back out on their word, it may truly cause you to question the integrity of human beings. You will watch people choose mediocre over exceptional time and time again, mostly due to skepticism or laziness. And it will make you sad. Because you will believe in them wholeheartedly.

Overall it is a fairly simple business structure, but that doesn't mean that it's easy. If you want to hit the jackpot without doing any work, good luck with that. You won't find that here.

BECAUSE WHEN OPPORTUNITY KNOCKS, WORK ANSWERS.

If you want the benefits of something, you also have to want the costs. If you want predictable and safe and want to shield yourself from any risk, entrepreneurship, in general, is not for you. Still, the risk in starting a side hustle network marketing business is minuscule in comparison to any other startup.

I cannot guarantee your success, but I can guarantee that if you plug in with the right company that aligns with your values and vision, network marketing will change your life for the better because nobody can ever take away the real-life skills and relationships you will develop.

> *Life is too short not to try things.*

Fakepreneur

To properly understand the network marketing opportunity, we need to discuss the difference between owning a business and owning a job.

When I saw my name on that first business license and the title of "CEO & Owner" next to it, I was filled to the brim with pride and joy. Corporate America would never call the shots in my life. It fed my ego to share with people at BBQs and cocktail parties that I owned a personal training business.

But the reality was that the "business" owned me.

Whether you're a nanny earning $35 per hour, a hairstylist earning $65 per hour, a personal trainer earning $80 per hour, an attorney earning $500 per hour, or a business coach earning $2,000 per hour, being self-employed will never set you free. You can't unplug and continue to earn a paycheck. Your financial stability is always tied to the amount of time you put in, which means you are constantly deciding between servicing your clients to pay the bills or spending time with your family.

- **Here's what a business is *not*:** anything that requires you to do a certain something to earn a certain something.
- **Here's what a business *is*:** creating systems that produce income while you're sleeping.

Let's say you own a dog-walking business. It starts out with you single-handedly walking dogs for $30 per hour. This is not a business yet. If you break your ankle, you're out of work. Eventually, the word gets out about your fantastic services, so you need to hire someone to help you walk dogs—an employee. After paying professionals to legally set you up with the infrastructure for employees, someone refers you the perfect first employee. After you train her, she is off to the races. Hooray! A step in the right direction.

But now you are also responsible for managing an employee, payroll, scheduling, and not to mention the new taxes you won't be able to hide from. For the sake of demonstration, let's imagine this employee is everything you could ever hope for. She is punctual, reliable, and likable. Doggies love her. She loves her job, and will be loyal to you for years. However, one employee is not enough to leverage your time. You have to continue walking dogs at the same rate in addition to your employee to make more money. Now the whole neighborhood raves about your services, so you continue to add more employees to keep up with demand. And then another problem: Mr. Johnson's terrier doesn't like your new employee. He wants YOU! With careful attention, you eventually wean doggie dependency and make the pass off. Hopefully, at some point, you are able to stop walking dogs entirely as you deal with more of the backend such as managing employees, marketing, customer service, and so on. Still, if you take a three-week vacation, will everything fall apart?

It's not a work ethic thing for most people—it's a lack of the right business model in their lap.

Until you have duplication and systems in place that do not require your presence in order to continue running, you do not have a business.

Please stop saying you own business if you really just own a job.

How Does it Work

"When I talk to people about it, they are always skeptical it's a pyramid scheme."

I was sitting on a couch with an Olympic hopeful. He had been using our product line for several years to improve his performance and recovery as he vied to become a professional athlete. He was also living paycheck to paycheck, considering buying an engagement ring on credit, driving Uber to make ends meet, and was $45,000 in debt. I looked him straight in the eyes and asked, "Is that what you think? Do you think this is all some big scam that I've been pouring my heart into for seven years?"

Many people don't take the time to understand how direct selling works, so they skip over it as a viable opportunity and inaccurately label it a "pyramid" or "Ponzi" scheme. Let's just get this out of the way right here, right now: pyramid schemes are illegal. People throw cash in a pot and there is no actual product being sold. I'm going to explain why direct selling is absolutely not a pyramid scheme shortly, but first we need to understand what direct selling *actually* means.

Direct selling is an industry where there is retail product being sold through direct distributors. Independent contractors (or representatives or distributors) have the opportunity to sell a product directly to their contacts and earn a commission for doing so. Most direct selling companies also allow participants to sponsor other sales representatives. They constitute a rep's "downline," and their sales have the ability to generate income for those above them; their "upline". It is most similar to the franchise business model because the product and systems are already proven and in place for success, just waiting for the right leaders to grab hold. Instead of a more traditional way of retailing product, distributors are the marketers, and in turn, they get compensated for their marketing efforts.

I was recently away in Palm Springs for a girls weekend, and we were all gathered around the pool, sipping on bubbly while complaining about our never-ending battle with body odor and the lack of deodorant options that:

A. Actually work, and

B. Aren't full of chemicals that could give us cancer.

One of the gals raved about the natural deodorant she had been using. We sampled the goods and three of us ordered it right away using the link to the retailer's website. Now, I'm happy because I have an all-natural deodorant that makes me smell of orange and bergamot. My friend is happy because she had the satisfaction of paying it forward and helping three more people be less stinky. The retailer of the product was the only person who benefited monetarily from this referral, and I'm sure she is happy about that too. If this deodorant had been distributed through direct selling and my friend had been a distributor, she could have earned a commission for that exact same scenario by sending us a link to her very own website. Win, win, win.

Direct selling is the most organic way to promote solutions as it spreads awareness of products through personal recommendation and experience.

My friend barely had to sell us on it—she simply shared her experience and let us try it for ourselves. How basic is that?!

> *Life is too short to let skepticism*
> *overshadow the truth.*

Common Objections

No business opportunity is more misunderstood and criticized than network marketing. At its best, it is seen as something stay-at-home moms do for social hour or something strange Uncle Bob does to build his fortune. At its worst, it is perceived as a cult full of shady people who invite you to nondescript meetings to sell you toilet paper. But once you get past the old-school attitudes and misconceptions, you uncover this gem for what it truly is: the keys to a Lamborghini. A vehicle for change. A vehicle for hope. A vehicle for freedom.

Of course, you have to actually get *inside* the Lambo and drive it in order to reap the thrill. Below, I've unpackaged common objections to help you overcome any lingering stereotypes you could still be harboring.

It's too late/saturated.

Saturation is impossible because every day new people are born or turn 18, therefore adding new potential teammates to the pool of prospects. There are always more people to impact if the product is solid and is providing a solution to a relevant problem.

It doesn't work.

According to the Direct Selling Association, in 2015, the direct sales industry grossed more than $36 billion in retail sales in the United States alone with more than 20 million people in the States involved. Obviously, network marketing works. Success or failure is determined by the amount effort one puts into their business. Many bloggers, Etsy affiliates, and other home business owners don't do well or quit too, but you don't hear people saying blogging and Etsy don't work.

It's a pyramid scheme.

A pyramid scheme is illegal since it provides no products or services, and it pays according to the number of recruits. Legal network marketing programs offer quality products or services that are sold to consumers. Recruiting new members allows for increased income based on the volume of sales, with team sales volume—not the number of recruits—being the important factor in calculating income. Legitimate direct sales companies also adhere to laws, such as publishing average income statistics, no inventory requirements, and refund options.

I was recently talking to a sales manager of a multi-million dollar startup. He's a corporate guy; been building up the ranks for 30-plus years. He described his bonus structure and how he earns more if his sales team earns more. This is no different whatsoever than network marketing. In fact, it's a well-established business practice, and people don't go calling biotech startups "pyramid schemes."

You need to get in on the "ground floor" to have success.

Many ground-floor members make nothing while many who come in years later make a fortune. I joined my company 15 years after they were founded. Personally, I liked that there was a solid track record and a foundation laid by those who came before me. The business model works regardless of what time you start with it.

My spouse isn't on board.

The first time I earned over $4,000 in a month, I finally got James' attention. It took $4,000 to even get a head turn from that guy! He loved the products but had a hard time believing it was worth the effort. At one point, I had to sit him down to sincerely share the vision I had and why it meant so much to me. He became very encouraging after hearing my heart, but he still did not step into building the business as my partner for several more years.

It isn't common that both spouses see the opportunity or catch the vision at the same time. Be patient, and march forward with unwavering belief. Do not let your spouse be your excuse.

Only the guy at the top makes money.

This argument more accurately describes a job. How often does a minimum wage worker become the CEO?

One of the things I love most about network marketing is that your income is related to effort, not position. No matter when you join or where you are in the organization, you have a fair chance to earn what you're after. There's no rigid hierarchy, no union stopping you from advancing too quickly, no wage caps. Really, there are no restrictions on your success except any you impose on yourself. You will get out of it what you put into it.

There are very few people who make a lot of money.

It's true that not everyone succeeds in network marketing. Bear in mind that this is also true in the traditional retail sales model. The 2 to 10 percent of network marketers earning big money are the same 2 to 10 percent who work consistently on their businesses. More impact = more income.

Not everyone wants to do what it takes to make a lot of money, which accounts for the remaining 90 percent. Many people simply enjoy earning some extra "mailbox" money to pay for things like gas, groceries, and gifts. This is perfectly OK. It leaves the door wide open for you to achieve the success you desire.

I don't have the right personality for this.

I've been around long enough to witness every single type of personality excel in this business. I am an introvert, I'm not particularly outgoing, I'm not super warm and fuzzy, I don't like big crowds or being around people for too long, and it's not in my nature to strike up a conversation with everyone I come across. But I'm making it happen because I have other strengths I put to work. Build your confidence by focusing on your unique strengths.

I don't know enough people.

I didn't know the vast majority of people I work with on my team before I started my business. Most of them did not go to school with me or know me for years—they got introduced to me by people who went to school with me or knew me.

For example, in 2012 an acquaintance through Facebook reached out to order our top fat-loss program. He bought it from my website, and despite my best efforts to follow up, I never heard from him...until one year later. He reached back out and said he'd been watching my success through the lens of social media. He was opening a CrossFit gym and wanted to talk about the opportunity. We met, he signed up, and we started working together on the business. The very first person he introduced me to on the phone was a high school friend of his. She lived halfway across the country, but she and I connected very quickly. She tiptoed into the business and eventually would become one of the top leaders on our team.

When you stick and stay and grow along the way, the right champions will bump into you.

I'm not a salesperson.

First of all, this business is not about making a sale; it is about nurturing relationships and coaching people to success. Also, don't be ridiculous. Nobody is born a salesperson. It is a skill that can be learned by anyone. Like I covered in the last chapter, sales requires connecting with another human being and offering a solution to a problem. To get great at sales, you must master the art of connection and storytelling.

> *Life is too short to toss aside the keys to a Lamborghini when you need to get somewhere quickly.*

 REFLECTION SECTION

Which- if any- of these objections do you find yourself battling? What will you do to change your mindset about it?

Choosing the Right Company

There was never a question in my mind whether the company I'm with was the right fit or not. The products worked, the compensation plan was generous, and above all, the culture was built upon the utmost integrity both on the corporate and distributorship level.

I was a believer.

Now that I've been in the industry awhile, I've noticed a common trend of people hopping between different companies as fast as they change hairstylists. To avoid that, let's make sure you start with the right company from the get-go. Below are three major aspects to keep in mind when you consider a company before going all-in.

1. Products

To build lasting wealth, you'll need to choose a product that is consumable. When I run out of skincare, I buy more. When I run out of supplements, I buy more. When I run out of makeup, I buy more. I don't run out of jewelry or purses or kitchen supplies often enough to warrant a regular purchasing habit. Not that making money with such items is impossible, you just don't have a ton of consistency.

You'll also want to choose a product you personally use and believe in. This is not about selling; it is about sharing. Your experience on products will be your best marketing tool. And it should be something you're extremely interested in because you will be talking about it *a lot*.

Do your due diligence. Try different products from different companies if you have to. Dig into who creates the products and how the products are formulated. Find something you love. Listen to testimonies. Choose something that will make a lasting difference in people's lives.

2. Plan

When I was introduced to my company, I didn't do much research on the compensation plan. I knew it had been working for 15 years, and I personally met countless people who were making respectable income with it, including a handful of seven-figure earners all across the nation. That was all I needed to know. But perhaps you are more skeptical or want to do more research than I did, which is totally understandable. My advice is to ask the person who will potentially sponsor you to sit down with you and go into detail about how you get paid. Will there be minimums you have to hit? What is the commission and bonus structure? Are there auto-shipping requirements? Can you lose your "status" at any point?

Also, make sure the company is a member of the Direct Selling Association (DSA; you can search the directory at DSA. org). Members of the DSA have pledged to abide by a strict Code of Ethics that outlines a high set of standards for interactions with both sellers and customers. Many of these are voluntary standards that exceed the requirements of any regulations created by the Federal Trade Commission (FTC) or mandated by federal or state law. In my opinion, any credible direct sales company will be a member.

3. People

When someone asks me whether I think they should join company A or company B, I highly recommend they attend an event for each to get a feel for the leadership and culture. *This. Is. Everything.* Many network marketing companies have phenomenal products and lucrative compensation plans—but organizations rise and fall on leadership. The people are what make the difference! Ask yourself, would you "do life" with these people? Do they share similar values? Are they walking the walk? Are they deeply committed to your success? Spend time with them. How is their character? Are their hearts in the right place? Being around the leaders in my company makes me want to be a better person. I couldn't ask for anything more.

Don't take this decision lightly. Although not impossible, it is tough to switch companies once you have dug your heels in.

Keep it Classy

WE'RE GONNA BE RICH!!!

I loved eavesdropping on my mom's living room vitamin parties. It was the 90's, and she got involved with a booming MLM business. She earned a cruise, got our family healthy, and contributed a part-time income from home while raising five kids. Eventually, life happened, and she moved on, but I always had a very positive impression of direct sales.

Back then there was no social media, and marketing was a totally different ball game. Building a business was entirely belly-to-belly; fliers on bathroom stalls, home phone calls, and maybe the occasional use of an exciting new technology called email. Nowadays, if you are building *any* kind of business and you don't utilize social media for free marketing and networking, I have no words.

On the other hand, why anyone would live up to the cheesy, sales-y stereotype of a network marketer on their social media also leaves me dumbfounded.

In an industry with a barrier to entry considerably low, some bad apples operate their businesses poorly either because of unawareness, or they simply have not been coachable. As part of my mission is to bring excellence to the network marketing profession, I am going to make it extremely clear what *not* to do before we get deeper on what to do.

Please keep it classy, and don't do these things:

- **DON'T add friends to a Facebook group without consent:** When someone has expressed interest in your product or business, then by all means, add them to a private group. But don't just go adding all your friends who you *think* will be interested. This is a surefire way to look like you don't actually care or that you're too lazy to share with them individually. Instead, personally invite them to take a further look at what you're doing and how you might be able to help them.

- **DON'T post about your company incessantly:** It's important that people know what you do, but it's also important they know you have a life outside of your company. It just isn't attractive to be over-the-top-zealous-crazy-eyelash-queen. People buy YOU before they buy any product or business.

- **DON'T show distasteful, poorly photographed images:** Wear appropriate clothing for your before/after pictures. Use a decent camera with good lighting. Don't take selfies in your bra and in your messy bathroom. Unless you want to attract creepy 45-year-old dudes with profile pictures of their cat to your business, really not recommended. Make it look professional, and people will treat you like a professional.

- **DON'T make your profile picture your company's logo:** Network marketing is a personal business. Be a person. Be you. Not an irrelevant, fanatical robot.

- **DON'T send private messages with four paragraphs of information—before interest is even shown:** If I get a private message out of nowhere with "Hi, I want to tell you about my company..." and it goes on with incessant facts and stories, good luck ever getting my business. Instead, send a message asking, "Hey, have you found a need for better shampoo in your life?" And I will tell you yes or no. And the conversation will either continue or not. You need to qualify a customer if you want to get good at sales.

- **DON'T tell people about your "new thing":** If you call your company or product a "thing" instead of by the actual name, I will immediately know you have little belief in what you're doing. You're trying to hide from the stereotype of MLM, and instead, you are just contributing to it. Make sure you're promoting something you believe in.

- **DON'T try to recruit a high-income earner from another company:** It happens on the regular. People reach out to share their opportunity with me. I guess I can't blame them—they're hungry for success! However, if they have been watching my life, even just a little bit, they would know there is absolutely no way I would ever consider another company. Not even a chance.

- **DON'T switch companies every nine months:** I understand if the first company was a bad fit, and after you caught the vision, you moved on to a company more aligned with your values. But if you are on your third company in the three years I've known you, it is a big red flag. Building a direct sales business takes *time* like any other business! If you keep jumping ship, you will never gain traction, and you will lose more and more credibility each time. Stick and stay!

- **DON'T promote two companies at once:** I use products from four different direct sales companies, but I am only a distributor for one of them. The other three I refer out, and the products do not compete with my products. There is no shortage of fantastic products distributed through direct selling, but promoting two companies at once is a recipe for disaster. It screams short-term, only-in-it-for-the-money commitment. Not followable. Not trustworthy. Choose what you are most interested in, the product you love, and where you admire the leadership. Stay focused on a long-term vision.

- **DON'T complain, use profanity, or write really extreme views on religion/politics on social media:** It's a free world with free speech, but if you are looking to build a business and attract people to what you have, I recommend keeping these types of posts at bay. Ultimately, you're going to attract what you put out in the universe. Don't give people a reason not to work with you.

- **DON'T put a logo on a beater car:** Putting my company logo on my car has never been part of my marketing strategy. I'm proud of my company, but I personally would never track someone down for products because of a logo on their car. And I drive too fast. It certainly is a great way to get noticed, however, and many of my friends do it. You really never know! It could grant you a new customer or two. So if you wear your colors on your car, by all means, please act accordingly. When I see a logo on a beater car with dents and broken windows covered in duct tape, I cringe with remorse for the entire network marketing industry. And if you have a suitable vehicle, then please, please, please don't drive like a jerk-wad. People are watching.

Remember, the moment you choose to distribute a product, you are not just representing yourself, your family, and your company. You are representing the entire direct selling industry!

Be WORLD CLASS in all that you do.

Marketing 101

In 1994, a 30-year-old Wall Street computer science wiz quit his lucrative job to start an Internet company. His first step was to secure funding, so who did he approach? His parents, naturally. He sat them down and shared his vision. He told them there was a 70 percent chance they would lose their entire investment, which was a few hundred thousand dollars, and they did it anyway ... because they believed in him.

If Jeff Bezos can ask his family for a few hundred grand to sell books online, you can certainly ask your friends and family to support your vision. Of course, there is no guarantee they will say yes. To this day, nobody in my entire family buys products from me, but that's never stopped me. I keep sharing my story and marching forward.

The real work in getting your business off the ground is opening your mouth. If every one of your friends and family doesn't know what you're working on, you're doing something wrong. You must TALK TO PEOPLE. You cannot hide behind a computer screen or text messages. You have to open your mouth and share your products and vision face-to-face or over FaceTime if they live in another state. Belly-to-belly will never go away because this business is personal. It requires looking into people's eyes and telling them the possibilities you see for yourself—and more importantly, what you see for them.

Be Your Own Brand

" I'm not a businessman. I'm a business, man. "

—JAY Z

People won't buy into an idea or product if they can't get past the messenger—and that messenger is you. *You* are the business. By stepping into entrepreneurship, you must be hyper-aware of your own personal brand.

What do people think of when they think of you? Trustworthy? Put together? Authentic? Consistent? Bold? Or...are you sloppy? Always late? Hypercritical? Wishy-washy? Insecure? Potential customers pick up on this stuff, and they will gladly work with someone else if they are more attracted to that person.

Above all, your likelihood of success depends the most on your unshakeable belief in yourself and your company.

Hobbyist versus Business Builder

Perhaps you have read this far but still aren't convinced you have the bandwidth to take on an entirely new venture. I have a solution for you: start slow. There is no rule that you must build big or with speed. I was a "hobbyist" with my business for three years before I had that defining moment when I stepped into being a "business builder." There is something for everyone, and you can always move up or down with engagement depending on your desired outcome. Either way, it's important that I clarify the difference because often people expect a business-builder income when they are only willing to put in a hobbyist effort.

Here are a few characteristics that generally describe the difference between the two:

Hobbyist

- You love your company's products or service and are a regular consumer.
- You are interested in making extra "mailbox" money.
- You enjoy helping and encouraging others.
- You love the community and culture of your company and find it brings great value to your life.
- You attend events here and there when they work with your schedule.
- You may be open to turning your business into something bigger in the future, but the timing is not right for now.
- You're willing to invest three to five hours per week into your business.
- You're happy passing customer follow-ups on to your upline.
- You are more focused on sharing products than sharing the opportunity.
- You talk with your upline sponsor a few times per month.

Business Builder

- You love your company's products or service and are a regular consumer.
- You have a long-term mindset and are committed to intentionally building your business for a minimum of five years.
- Your goal is to become a Time Millionaire by first getting debt-free, then replacing your income from your current job, and finally living a freedom-based lifestyle earning a full-time income (whatever that may mean to you).

- You feel called to helping and coaching others towards success.
- You have an intense burning desire for growth both personally and professionally.
- You are absolutely sick and tired of one or many of these things: living paycheck to paycheck; never having enough to fund epic experiences and vacations; always having to ask permission for time off; your living situation; being at the beck and call of your manager (or clients!); having to drop your kids off at daycare; spending the majority of your week fighting traffic; not feeling as though you are regularly adding significance to people's lives; arguing with your spouse about money; not having enough for retirement or college savings; being too exhausted at the end of the day to give your best to your family; watching your children grow up through FaceTime; and/or living your life on the sidelines.
- You connect with the community and culture of your company and find the mission to be in alignment with your core values.
- You prioritize events into your calendar and attend every single event and training within a day's drive.
- You are fully committed to attending any national convention.
- You're willing to invest 10 to 15 hours per week into your business.
- You are always present on appointments with your upline mentor.
- You are equally focused on sharing products as you are on sharing the opportunity.

- You talk with your upline sponsor nearly every day and stay connected to the team.

Clearly, building your business to a high level is going to require more effort.

WHAT YOU PLANT, YOU WILL HARVEST.

> *Life is too short to do the minimum and expect the maximum.*

 REFLECTION SECTION

What are you willing and able to commit to right now? Do you fit in more as a "hobbyist" or a "business builder"?

Industry Future

If you've had a perfectly glazed Krispy Kreme donut, had a bite of a Big Mac, stayed at a Hilton hotel, or made a sweat angel at an Orangetheory Fitness, you've experienced the workings of a franchise business model. Franchising didn't gain traction until the 1950's, and by the 1960's, it was under the microscope for being accused of using deceptive sales practices and double-selling the same franchise territories to different persons. Eventually, in 1979, federal regulation came into play. The scrappy franchisors went away, and the legitimate players who complied with the FTC regulations changed and became giants. In our present economy, franchising is recognized as a completely legal and lucrative industry.

The same process that happened in franchising is happening with network marketing. The first network marketing business began in the 1930's in the United States, and just as any new industry emerges, there have been serious growing pains. The 2016 FTC settlements with Herbalife and Vemma introduced new federal guidelines and regulations that will become the standard for all direct sales companies to comply with in the near future. Ethical companies willing to work with these guidelines will become the Subway's and Chick-fil-A's of the industry. Change is happening, and it is very good change.

When I am attempting to put together an outfit for an event, I scroll through fashion influencers on Instagram and click on their links to buy. When I am researching travel, I scroll through travel influencers on Instagram and book hotels based on their photos. When I am in need of a professional for things like photography or beauty services, I check them out on Instagram before committing. Shoot, I just bought my baby's entire nursery off a photo on Instagram!

The world is more connected than ever, and with the explosion of social media celebrities promoting the heck out of clothes they wear, the equipment they use, the hotels they frequent—all for a commission to do so—it is becoming widely acceptable and common to sell products you believe in.

So, why wouldn't you do the same?

Additionally, there are huge tax benefits for having a home-based business. Many W-2 employees give themselves an immediate raise because of the eligible tax write-offs you benefit from being a business owner for things such as their home office, supplies, travel, and so on.

> *Disclaimer: I am not a tax professional. Please consult a qualified CPA for details on how business ownership can benefit your exact situation.*

Direct selling hasn't even scratched the surface of its potential. People need supplemental income. People need to protect their hard-earned money. People need significance; to be part of a movement, something bigger than themselves.

YOUR YES TO BECOME A TIME MILLIONAIRE
WILL CHANGE YOUR FUTURE.

> *Life is too short to miss out.*

If Not ... Then What?

I started my personal training business right out of college when the economy was tanking in 2008. I just turned off the news and haven't turned it on to this day. Despite the gloomy financial forecast, my business thrived. So much so that I needed to expand. I fantasized about owning a gym, and the dream was to build it right on Lake Union, the centerpiece of Seattle. On a weekly basis, I ran the 6.2-mile loop around the lake convincing myself, "Someday, I will open a waterfront gym here on the lake and train my clients to the sound of gentle waves crashing and pink sunrises behind the mountains." Plus, I heard some company called Amazon was building offices in the neighborhood and they would likely fuel local business (wasn't that an understatement!).

One exhausting day, I got a crazy idea to explore waterfront property on Craigslist, and on the very first search, on the very first page, there it was: 2,000 square feet of sweeping lake views. Could it be? Was this my sign? It was perfect. I had to have it. There was no time for thinking, only time for doing. First action step: find a business partner. The thought of undertaking this on my own scared the living daylights out of me. Instead of considering prospects that may align with my core values, I chose the first person that had a background in fitness and access to money.

As I mentioned in Chapter 2, six short months later, despite business couples counseling and multiple failed efforts to repair, we broke up. He got the gym and $50,000 of debt. I got put on the street and was responsible for $25,000 of debt.

It was the biggest learning lesson of the decade. My "MBA," as I like to say.

Although I didn't get fancy letters after my name, I beg to wager I learned far more from this on-the-job training than I ever would've learned in a lecture. I discovered the ins and outs of running a storefront business and why I would likely never open one again. Not only was the decision bad to partner with this guy, but it was also a bad decision on my part to even open the gym in the first place based on my long-term vision for my life. We had no unique offerings and no plans for duplication.

Days after my business partner locked me out of the gym, I was vehemently writing up a business plan for a new gym. I was going to open one to prove how much more awesome I was. I even went as far as finding business partners (again!) and touring several commercial spaces.

A few weeks into this quest, I found myself sitting upright on the velvet couch next to the crackling fire in James' bachelor pad with my MacBook on my lap asking: "Do I really, truly want to open a gym again? To go through the whole process all over? Commit to thousands upon thousands of more dollars in debt? Open doors at 5 a.m. and stay until 10 p.m. closing? Pay multiple electricity bills and wash towels during the only spare hours I'm not at the gym?

Deal with flaky trainers who always put on the Metallica Pandora station? Is that *really* what I want to do the next 20 years?"

Hmm, no. Nope. No way.

I needed a plan. And so do you.

If not network marketing, then what? What is it going to be? You must determine how you are going to create time for the things you love most. Driving UBER on the side won't do it. Selling stuff on Craigslist won't do it. Picking up extra shifts won't do it.

Find a company you love and a mentor doing what you want to do in the industry you want to be in and go for it!

> *Life is too short to let your ego get in the way.*

Hopefully, after reading and reflecting your way through the first four chapters you are far more confident in yourself and in this business model. To bring it all together, let's dive into *how* you will build the ultimate side hustle by first getting clear on your goals and vision.

CHAPTER 5

GOAL SETTING THAT WORKS

"Meh"

When you come back from a trip around the world, everyone assumes that it must suck to be home. That life is basically over. Goodbye unplanned dance parties in your underwear and hiking through white sand dunes on a Wednesday. Hello predictably unruly traffic from 7 to 10 a.m. and 2 to 8 p.m. each day Monday through Friday (I only leave my house from 10 to 2, just in case you ever want to meet up).

I try to bring joy and light wherever I go. I really do try. Even when I don't feel like being social (common for us introvert-types), I fortunately have enough maturity to understand that if I make decisions solely based on my feelings, I will go nowhere and have no friends and make no difference. So, when I was recently making the 20-minute trip to the city for a networking event, I had my plan in place to get my energy right: pop music and caffeine.

My run-ins with humanity on this particular day really got me thinking about how many people must be living in quiet desperation. It was a beautiful sunny Saturday morning, and out of the hundreds of people I greeted at the event that day, maybe eight mustered the courage to make eye contact with me. And out of those eight, three smiled. I overheard a good handful of people use the phrase, "Oh, it's just one of those days." I wondered how often "those days" must come around. Usually the excuse people make for their disdain is the moody Pacific Northwest (PNW) weather. But not this time. There was no excuse. It wasn't a Monday morning, and it wasn't grey. People were just numb. I even ran into an acquaintance and she literally told me her life was "Meh."

I needed a break from the Seattle Freeze, so I walked into a coffee shop and the barista asked me how it was going. I said "Great! It's a great day to be alive." He acknowledged my enthusiasm and replied, "Awesome, we need more people around here with that attitude." You don't say...

I have been discouraged. I have been frustrated. I have been impatient. I have been unsatisfied. I have been anxious. Life is not meant to be easy. "You will have trouble," He said. But I have never been meh, surviving instead of thriving, working towards the weekend instead of working towards a vision.

Meh is the byproduct of the mediocrity vortex society sucks you into if you aren't intentional with your life.

Many people have meh lives, and my deepest desire is that you never get anywhere close to living a meh life. Not always, but more often than not, I'm excited to go to bed early, because I'm excited to wake up early and continue working on my dreams. I wasn't born some super-peppy Pollyanna. I am just sincerely jazzed about the projects I get to work on because I took the time to build residual income and not live on someone else's schedule.

> *Life is too short to be meh.*

Resist the Drift

Goals keep you out of "meh."

But there's one major problem: most people don't write down goals. Most people just drift through life with no sincere direction due to a lack of self-awareness. Or fear. Those are the two biggest reasons people choose their couch over their dreams. Have you ever met someone who had no idea what they wanted to "be" and kept going back to college? Society teaches us that our worth and identity is defined by our career label. That the perfect job choice will lead to happiness. Society sells the sizzle of sexy titles and accolades.

SOCIETY LOVES TO KEEP YOU IN A STATE OF BUSY AND COMPARISON.

Here's the path society starts selling you the day you watch your first TV commercial, the path that ultimately leads to the drift:

- Spend the first 18 years of your life in school. Most of that time, you deal with bullies and try to measure up to your classmates. Society wants you to believe you're unworthy.

- Commit the next 4 years of your life investing your precious time and funding into a college degree, which quite possibly you may never use to make money.

- Work for free (i.e., an internship) and just maybe you will earn yourself a paid salary.

- Live in a big city because that's where the best companies to work for are located. And guess what? You land a job because of your previous free labor! Awesome! Except the starting salary is $70,000 per year. This won't cover your boutique fitness classes *and* your doggy day care. You hate having to choose, so...

- Go back to school to earn a master's degree. You are barely scraping by in the big city on a regular salary and surely more letters after your name will lead to a pay raise. It will be worth all the student loan debt. Society said so.

- Continue fighting traffic five days a week and dealing with competitive coworkers and bosses, always having to watch your back because everyone is in it for themselves. Just keep your head down and climb that ladder.

- Squeeze in just enough time to swipe through the dating app and meet the love of your life.

- Spend at least a year planning your wedding. Maybe two. Save up so you can impress a lot of people you barely know. In fact, just put it on the credit card. What's a little more debt, eh?

- Get married. And since all the planning was for your bachelorette party and cake flavors, spend the first year or two navigating unfamiliar territory (i.e., fighting over how to load the dishwasher, resulting in someone sleeping on the couch).
- The clock is ticking; it's time to procreate! Baby on the way! Marital issues? What marital issues? Didn't you hear me... baby on the way!!!
- Now the balancing act: someone needs to raise the kiddos, and someone needs to provide. Wait...both need to provide. Dual income is necessary to maintain lifestyle and to keep up with the Kardashians. Life gets very hectic. Health goes by the wayside. Sleep is a luxury preserved for rich people. Like that annoying stay-at-home mom Mrs. Petrie. And seriously, is her family going to Hawaii AGAIN?
- Marriage becomes more like a roommate situation. Haven't had sex in three weeks. Or three months. Can't remember. It's more of a business partnership, these days. Just gotta get through these, uh, next 25 years. Or at least make it to that Vegas weekend getaway in four months.
- Can't handle the lack of passion anymore. The "D" word starts being brought up more and more....

Believe it or not, I have met people that have followed this exact path! Maybe there are bits and pieces from this scenario you can relate to and you're mad at me right now for pointing them out.

Let go of the offense. Life is too short to be offended.

OFFENSE IS LIKE BUILDING A BRICK WALL BETWEEN YOU AND YOUR DREAMS.

You can't get around it, and you can't slide through it. You can only bulldoze it and then never let it creep in again. You must get to the root of the issue and start chopping it down.

Here's the thing: I care about you—deeply. It's why I'm writing this book in the first place. I genuinely want you to succeed by providing you with these tools. What I do not want is for you to run to your group of girlfriends from middle school to dish about your problems looking for an, "Oh, honey, join the club!"

Don't join the club. Resist the club. Being a member of said club will cause you sleeplessness and anxiety knowing the best years of your life are being spent building someone else's dream instead of building memories with those you love most. And for what? Good health insurance and a false idea of a secure paycheck? Society loves to sell you this dirty little lie.

IF YOU WANT THINGS TO BE DIFFERENT, YOU MUST BEGIN TO SEE THINGS DIFFERENTLY.

Be different! Don't be like most people. Most people in our nation are miserable. Most people live for the weekend and care more about their football team than their own dreams. Most people spend a day's worth of time in front of the TV every week. Most people hate their jobs, meaning they hate the majority of their time awake. Most people work longer than eight hours per day. Most people earn less than a six-figure income. Most people are overweight, sleep deprived, and dehydrated. Most people accept life instead of *creating* life. Most people choose instant gratification instead of respecting opportunity cost. Most people are drifting through life.

There's another path that few will take, but it is wildly available to anyone who wants it. It will still be hard work, usually even harder. This exhilarating path is not so cut and dry. However, one thing I can guarantee is anyone who excels at this path knows what they want and why they want it. And when you have clarity on your goals, even if you don't know *how* the vision is going to happen, life falls into a state of flow. You wake up with a sense of why you are here and where you are going.

SIGNIFICANCE HAS NOTHING TO DO WITH TITLES AND EVERYTHING TO DO WITH VISION.

If you don't have a vision for your life, you will fall victim to the drift. You cannot be stuck in the drift if you want to be a Time Millionaire, so let's get to work on your vision.

> *Life is too short to choose the popular way over the superior way.*

Your Perfect Day

You are the architect of your life, and your goals are the blueprint. They are the stepping-stones that keep you accountable to your vision of becoming a Time Millionaire. The first step in formulating goals is not to focus on what you want to have, but to get clear on *how you want to live* each and every day.

I used to play this game called M-A-S-H-O with my girlfriends. All you need is a piece of paper and a pencil and you have the power in your hands to predict your future.

Essentially, you write out a list of life categories, such as where you will live, who you will marry, what your career will be, what car you will drive, how many kids you will have. You know, the notable accomplishments society tips their hat to. Then, by way of some number configuration, your entire future is determined. I practically always ended up living in a mansion, married to Justin Timberlake, mom to three kids, driving a Lexus, and being a pop star. Or a lawyer. That sounded respectable too. If by some atrocity I ended up living in an outhouse or driving a station wagon, I pleaded for a do-over because that just simply did not align with my vision. I was a girl who knew what she wanted, and who clearly watched way too much MTV. As an adult, though, it wasn't until a few years ago when I sat down and outlined my perfect day that I had breakthrough on who I wanted to be and how I wanted to live.

Here is my perfect day:

6 A.M.: Wake up naturally
6 TO 8 A.M.: Pray, visualize, journal, read, write, etc.

8 TO 10 A.M.: Workout, shower

10 A.M. TO 1 P.M.: Create content (write articles, posts, book material, and music)

1 TO 4 P.M.: Take appointments, communicate and coach my team

4 TO 6 P.M.: Read, cook dinner, go on a walk with Jamesy

6 TO 9 P.M.: Family time

9 P.M.: Read in bed and fall asleep

By writing this out, it solidified that my fight for financial freedom was not just to fund lavish experiences and write big checks at uppity soirees. No...my fight was for the time to live healthfully, peacefully, and to use my gift to add value to people's lives. Every. Single. Day. Of course, not every day plays out this idealistically. Often there are errands to run and evening commitments and business trips to be made. But when I first got clear on my perfect day and wrote it down, I was living zero out of seven days a week like this. Now I live about five out of seven days per week in my flow. Perhaps you noticed that my perfect day does include working. Not only do I enjoy most aspects of building my business, I believe we are called to work and we are happiest when we are working.

Hustling smarter is not about not working; it is about doing work that allows you to use your gift while creating residual income so money never comes between you and what matters most.

> *Life is too short to not wake up excited.*

REFLECTION SECTION

Describe your perfect day, similar to what I did above. Remember this is your PERFECT day. You have all the time in the world and money in the bank. The more specific you get with your itinerary, the easier it is to visualize it into reality.

Here are a few questions you can start with:

- What time do you wake up?
- Who is beside you?
- Where do you live?
- What does your home look and feel like?
- What do you do when you first get up?
- What are you wearing when you head out the door?
- What is on the agenda for the day?
- How many hours will you work?
- What work will you be doing?
- What will you do when you finish work for the day?

Setting Life Goals

Ok, NOW it's time to uncover what you want to have, do and experience. This is when goal setting gets *really* fun!

When many Americans are returning socks from Grandma the week between Christmas and New Years, I am well underway with my yearly process of free-writing my life goals. I set goals annually, and I revisit them daily. I read them, re-write them, pray over them, and call them in. Whatever comes to my mind, and nothing is too big or too small. The silly, the ridiculous, and the intimidating are all welcome. And they are embraced with open arms.

Because of this intentional goal setting process, I have seen many dreams realized...

- I ran 26.2 miles under 4 hours 29 minutes on a perfect, sunny October day to celebrate my 26th birthday.
- I graduated college in three years.
- I sang at Cowboy Stadium in front of 25,000 people in a choir with Michael W. Smith.
- I rode a hot air balloon at sunrise in ancient Cappadocia, Turkey.
- I clapped for the sunset on Ipanema Beach as it dropped behind Sugarloaf Mountain in Rio de Janeiro.
- I cruised Lake Como on a vintage Riva. A moment so classic it could be suited for George Clooney himself.
- I danced under the sparkling Eiffel Tower at night with my closest friends and family.

- I rode a camel at sunset in the North African desert with D & B and Fufi the drone. This was before Fufi got seized by Moroccan authorities.
- I sunbathed all day on a naturalist beach in Ibiza. James kept his shorts on. Rebel.

These life goals are specific and focused on highlight-reel experiences. Sometimes goals come and go, and I realize they were never that important to me. But sometimes I can't get certain goals off my mind, and they just stick around until they are accomplished. That's when I know they are from up above.

YOUR VISION AND YOUR GOALS ARE WHAT GET YOU OUT OF BED IN THE MORNING WITH EXCITEMENT AND ANTICIPATION.

Dreams energize you. Vision is the mental image of what could be in the future, and formulating your vision is part of the work. You can't put your hands to the plow if you don't have the faintest clue what kind of garden you're growing. As we covered in Chapter 1, nothing happens without purpose behind it. And purpose is attached to and clarified by vision.

When you let your brain run wild and free, it's amazing what ideas will come out. You can get inspiration from blogs, magazines, books, Pinterest and Instagram. One of my favorite books of all-time is *The Circlemaker* by Mark Batterson. In the book, Mark talks about hiking the Inca Trail with his son. All of a sudden, I wanted to do it too. Even though I despise camping and squat toilets and mosquitoes, it inspired me and Jamesy to take action, and that's how we kicked off the South America portion of #GarnersGoGlobal.

What we make public becomes a binding commitment. I want to challenge you to send an "I'm serious...no, really!" message to the universe by posting three of your life goals on Facebook or Instagram. Use the hashtag #timemillionairebook so we can cheer each other on. Setting goals is great, but being accountable for them kicks it up a notch.

> *Life is too short to settle.*

 REFLECTION SECTION

Write down anything, everything, and anyone that you want to do, meet, see, and/or experience in your lifetime. Keep thinking, and think hard. Don't feel the need to put a date on these goals. Just write down *everything* that comes up for you. Remove all limits.

To really get this exercise flowing, start by filling in the blank: Ever since I can remember, I have always dreamed about _____.

- Swimming with dolphins
- Taking a selfie at the pyramids
- Relaxing in the Blue Lagoon
- Spending Christmas with the whole family in Hawaii
- Writing a book
- Seeing Michael Jackson in concert (one can dream...)

These are just some ideas to get your dream-flow going! What can't not happen in your lifetime?

Reverse Engineering

Now that you are clear on how you want to live your day-to-day and you have a big-picture idea of the experiences you are dead set on having in your lifetime, it's time to break down the steps required to get there.

A dream written down with a date becomes a goal.
A goal broken down into steps becomes a plan.
A plan backed by action (AND FAITH!) makes your dreams come true.

If you've been discouraged with goal setting in the past, you were probably so focused on a specific outcome that when it didn't happen in the timeframe you expected, you lost faith. I see it happen in business all the time: "My goal is to earn $10,000 per month by this time next year so I can leave my job foreva and eva!!"

"Great!" I say. "So what are you committed to actually doing or changing in order to hit that target? Are you going to share your story with ten people per day? Are you going to invite a hundred people over the next three months to meet your mentor?" THESE are the goals that move the ball down the field.

The other problem I have seen time and time again with goal setting is that people write down exhaustive lists of changes they want and they become overwhelmed, leading to complete inaction on any of the goals.

Does a list like this look familiar?

- Learn to speak Spanish.
- Travel abroad.
- Get a promotion.
- Lose thirty pounds.
- Pay off debt.
- Stop drinking.
- Run a marathon.
- Make a career change.
- Start a family.
- Buy a house.

Bill Gates once said, "We always overestimate the change that will occur in the next two years and underestimate the change that will occur in the next ten. Don't let yourself be lulled into inaction."

To avoid overwhelm, I am going to teach you how to laser in and focus on what matters most in this season of your life.

Here's an example of my current one-year goals:

- **Health:** Gain no more than twenty-five pounds with pregnancy.
- **Career:** Finish, launch, and market this book to get into the hands of 10,000-plus people.
- **Financial:** Earn $500,000-plus in household income.
- **Personal:** Host a small group bible study at my house two times per month.

At the end of this section, your reflection will prompt you to write down your own goals. Once you have done this, I want you to write out two action steps you can take immediately for each goal. Having an end-goal in mind is great, but you must also focus on habits or actions you are committed to taking, opposed to the outcomes you want.

HABITS YOU CAN CONTROL;
OUTCOMES YOU CANNOT.

For example, if the outcome I want is to gain no more than twenty-five pounds during my pregnancy, it is more empowering to keep my focus on controllable factors like "workout a minimum of 20 minutes, six days per week" and "eat a minimum of 100 grams of protein daily." I can be clear about the weight I want to hit, but all I can *really* control is how often I'm moving and what I'm shoving in my mouth. Truly, that's it.

Here is another example of action steps for my career category:

Career goal: Finish, launch, and market this book to get in the hands of 10,000-plus people.
Career action steps:
1. Set a timer and write for 60 minutes every day until rough draft is finished.
2. Hire an editor and a designer.

By writing out the immediate action steps, you are already reverse-engineering your dreams and giving yourself clear next steps for what you need to do to turn the goal into reality.

> *Life is too short to leave your future to your memory.*

 **REFLECTION SECTION**

Start by dividing your goals into four categories: Health, Career, Personal, and Financial. Write only <u>one</u> goal for each category. You can certainly set goals with longer time frames, but I am going to have you start with one-year goals. After you have your four goals in place, write down <u>two</u> immediate action steps you can take that will move you towards fulfilling each goal within the next 365 days. When you're done, you should have a total of four goals and eight action steps written down.

Gratitude Entry

2014 felt like one of those years where I actually regressed. Of course, that wasn't true as the best growth happens in the valleys, but it sure felt like it in the moment. It was the first full year of marriage for me and Jamesy after coming off three months of honeymooning in 2013, and we were figuring out how to align our goals and work in sync as a couple. When the year was coming to an end, I still felt far away from the dreams burning in my heart. I needed new strategy.

On Christmas Day 2014, I curled up on my couch and wrote a journal entry dated December 25, 2015. It was written in the present tense, and it expressed gratitude for all the expectations I had for 2015: "I am so grateful for the $300,000 we were blessed with this year: it paid off our debt; it funded our world trip; and we were able to give away $30,000. I'm so grateful for the closeness and intimacy I have with James. Thank you for the incredible leadership in him. Thank you for the new champions on our team and in our lives."

I knew $300,000 was the magic number we needed to hit to pay off our remaining $55,000 in back taxes, fund our current lifestyle, and plan for our world trip. I believed it was possible, I just didn't know how.

WHEN THE *WHY* IS BIG ENOUGH,
THE *HOW* REVEALS ITSELF.

By the end of 2015, James and I had earned a combined 1099 income of $329,000. It was a miracle—nearly $100,000 more than we had ever earned in a year before. This was a tremendous blessing that I believe was made possible by our intention. When you are intentional about your vision, you start to think creatively. You take calculated risks because you know what got you *here* won't get you *there*. You work hard, and you pray hard.

That Christmas Day was the first time I had written a gratitude entry, and now it has become a staple in my routine. I write both a one-year entry and a ten-year entry annually. In my current season of life, I've been envisioning a scene in my mind so intimidating that I have NO idea how we are going to do it. All I have control over is putting the dream into writing and taking tiny steps every single day in that direction. I am fueled by these visions.

Once you have outlined your perfect day, made your list of life goals, and reverse-engineered the action steps for your current one-year goals, I want you to tie them all together with a gratitude entry. Allow yourself to truly believe achieving your goals is possible. Close your eyes and imagine what it is going to feel like when they are realized. This practice introduces you to visualization, an idea I will describe in more detail in the next section.

Your journey to become a Time Millionaire starts with your goals, your vision, your dreams.

So dream BIG, my friend.

> *Life is too short to dream small.*

 REFLECTION SECTION

Get that journal out, date it one year from today, and write a gratitude entry. Project what you want to see happen in your health, your finances, and your relationships. Get as detailed as you can.

Visualization

I hated riding the bus to school. My parents were raising five kids, so they weren't about to take each of us to our respective schools every day. I was unlike all of my friends, who were mostly only-children and their parents gave them curbside service in their luxury SUVs. No, it was the bus or bust for me. Besides, we had a purple family van from the 80s.

It was lose-lose trying to get to school with my ego intact.

Another reason I hated it was because I grew up in Washington State, right at the edge of the Columbia River Gorge. The majority of the time, I waited at the bus stop enduring sideways rain. No umbrella can protect you from sideways rain. If I tried to look pretty, my hair would blow into my lip-gloss and my high heels got showered with muddy splatter. This was before it was trendy to wear spandex and designer rain boots. If only...

But the reason I hated it the most was because I was on someone else's schedule. I felt like a sheep lining up to be herded into the daily grind of spending 75 percent of my day learning stuff that would never matter to me, 15 percent being social, and 10 percent learning stuff that did matter. Baaah! I really wished they would spend more time teaching me things that mattered, like when and how to use hyphens. I've had to Google it no less than twelve times already writing this book.

Also, I have always been predictably punctual. It didn't take long to discover that most people aren't. Most people are late. Including every bus driver I had from the age of 6 until 16. So there

I was, shivering at the bus stop, waiting for late people to transfer me to the land of pencil sharpeners and bureaucracy.

Years of my childhood were spent on that dreaded yellow bus with green faux leather seats, so I was determined to figure out a way to make my time useful. I'm a maximizer, which means wasting time is the next worse thing apart from death. I'm also an introvert by nature, so that ruled out talking to people outside of cute boys, of which there were few.

Instead, I commandeered my dad's oversized headphones, maxed out my Discman with the Michael Jackson *HIStory* album on repeat, and fantasized about my future life as a rock star. Every day, I mapped out my vision. I even started looking forward to the bus ride for the alone time getting lost in my ideas. Sometimes I would get embarrassed because my music was so loud, and I wondered if the other kids would notice I listened to so much Michael Jackson, known to my generation mostly for his court battles. I never actually cared enough, though, to turn it down. His precision in production and innovative writing mesmerized me. I choreographed dances routines in my head. Then, when imprisoned in classes like physics and calculus, I spent much of my formative years designing my stage wardrobe.

Teachers called it daydreaming. I called it visualization.

I earned a spot on the varsity soccer team my sophomore year in high school, and it was then that I learned my inkling for visualization was, in fact, a good thing. Our coach, Mr. Minder, was a very proud German. He loved riding his bicycle to work as much as he loved knocking back a few cold ones, hanging the German flag in his classroom, and coaching *futbol* with excellence.

My first time as a starter on the varsity roster, I was inducted into the pre-game ritual. All of us ladies with our ripe shin guards and high ponytails would gather in the locker room, find a spot to ourselves, and begin to meditate on the game ahead. The room was flooded with darkness as the lights were hit—then came the music.

For four minutes, we intently listened to *Carmina Burana: O Fortuna* blasting through the acoustics of the locker room. Of course, this song is by a German composer, and it is an absolute masterpiece. At every cymbal crash, I would picture myself driving past defenders and striking the ball into the net behind the goalie. I would envision the proud look on Mr. Minder's face when I dribbled through three lines of defense and made a perfect pass to my teammate who would knock it in the goal. He always seemed extra proud if we made the selfless act of passing it off to someone in a better position to score. I would envision "accidentally" tripping my opponent. The ref would have his back turned. I would envision the score at the end of the game, 3-0, us. I could already see my victory dance, ripping off my shirt and dropping to my knees, Brandi Chastain-style. I saw myself high-fiving my teammates and basking in the discouraged faces of the other team.

Imagine how we felt running on the field after that. Imagine the focus. The determination. The fire in our bellies to perform our best. To give it our all. That is the power of visualization.

I'm not quite so ruthless in my visualization practice these days. Now I utilize soft cello music. I often think about a specific scene where I am lying on a bank of freshly cut grass set along the

Italian coast with a baby on my chest and two little ones running around with James at our home for the summer. I see myself walking on stage and speaking life into a crowd of people. I imagine my book hitting #1 on the New York Times bestseller list. I dream about walking into our custom home with sweeping views and smiling as I look around and see rooms filled with friends and family laughing, eating, and enjoying the moment together. Connection. Impact. Creativity. Experience. These are the things I want more of in my life, so I spend time visualizing them.

THE HARDER YOU WORK, THE LUCKIER YOU GET.

And part of the work comes with your dedication to a visualization practice.

Whatever you want, visualize it. Let the imagery of your preferred future take you on a joy ride each and every day. Let your vision flood you with inspiration and confidence to act with courage in the face of inevitable challenges. Picture yourself succeeding at all of these goals and dreams you have put into writing. In doing so, it will boost your mood, confidence, and performance. And you will be that much closer to becoming a Time Millionaire.

> *Life is too short to leave your dreams to chance.*

Overcoming FOMO

When you have a decided heart and you say YES to achieving your goals *no matter what*, you will undoubtedly face opposition. This opposition can come in the form of fear, self-doubt, or the crippling need for control, as we addressed in the previous chapter. But oftentimes, it also simply comes in the form of distractions, leading you to make decisions with your time that are not in alignment with your goals. It is important to grasp that there is always an opportunity cost for every decision you make. James and I certainly got a dose of decision fatigue on #GarnersGoGlobal.

The hardest part about traveling the world with your spouse is not spending every waking moment together like one might think. I actually loved that part. It is the FOMO that haunts your every decision.

One thing James and I can certainly agree on is that we aren't fans of sifting through crowds to see another temple or cathedral or mosque. Those things are cool and all, but if we only have 4 hours in let's say Florence, it would be an easy decision to skip past the *duomo* and head straight to the Mercato Centrale, which is essentially a haven of Italian cuisine set up like a farmer's market. We are undeniable suckers for giant pieces of meat hanging from the ceiling washed down with local *vino rosso*.

Ultimately, you have to make a choice how to spend your time, and FOMO can come in hot. Which restaurant should we eat at? What does TripAdvisor say? How about the Instagram photos? Does the ambiance look exciting? Did we choose the best hotel in the best neighborhood? Do you reckon that's just a tourist trap? Even if it is, think it's worth it? Which spa service do you want to get? Is a third negroni prudent? Should we walk or taxi or bike or take the train? Maybe a boat? What about hopping over to that other country for the weekend? It's so close. Or should we just lay out in this sunshine all day and read? Is it wise to spend $300 on shoes? I probably won't ever see these shoes again!!!

I realize these are all absurd "first-world" qualms. I'm kind of embarrassed even sharing them. But the truth is that they are not far off from the typical daily struggles on our world trip. There will always be an opportunity cost.

WHEN YOU CHOOSE TO SPEND YOUR TIME DOING ONE THING, YOU ARE ACTIVELY CHOOSING NOT TO SPEND YOUR TIME DOING SOMETHING ELSE.

Take for example me right now: It's a Sunday morning at 10:50 a.m. I am choosing to sit my lululemon-clad behind in a local coffee shop to write these words. I still have my aviators on, even though I am sitting inside. They help me feel more stealthy, like I put on the One Ring and disappeared, sipping coffee while watching joy happen all around me. I am choosing to make progress on this book instead of the many other things I could be doing, like having brunch with friends. Pretty much everyone else in this shop is gabbing away with loved ones over avocado toast and yogurt parfait drizzled with gooey golden honey. (I told you I was spying.) Or I could be at a church service, although I read Proverbs last night, so that kind of counts. I could be working out, but I chose to set my alarm for 6 a.m. to hit SoulCycle with my hubs, eliminating the longing to be working out instead of typing away. I could also be doing income-producing activities, such as following up with my team and prospecting. But this book is important to get out to the public because I believe someone will read it and have a major breakthrough.

The point is that everything we do with time (and money) is a trade-off.

Each time I've gotten a new project underway, I eliminate just about anything that doesn't contribute to that goal outside of spending quality time with Jamesy, consistently hitting the gym, and reading a book to help me grow spiritually or as an entrepreneur. These are what I call non-negotiables. Don't get me wrong, I absolutely believe in rest and downtime. I enjoy a good movie! I have dinner with my friends! I call my family! However, I have wisdom with my yes's and no's. I understand no major headway can be made without sacrifice.

I remember early on in my journey, I had an event for my business on a Sunday afternoon. D & B had invited James and I to hang out, and we were having a fabulous time as always. As the fun heated up, I checked the clock and announced, "OK, guys, I have to take off!" This was followed by a bit of moaning and sadness (because I'm so awesome, *obvi*). At the time, I was just beginning my business journey, and there was no visible fruit for my friends to notice, but I explained, "Just watch. You'll understand soon." It's in those moments that we are tested. We are forced to make decisions between good and good.

Is it good to spend quality time with your dear friends? Of course it is.

Is it good to invest time into your budding business? Obviously.

You need to develop wisdom with where you put your energy when you are growing a creative project or business. You're going to have to make hard decisions between good and good. You are in a hustling season. You'll need to get rid of a few things now so you can have a lot more of them later.

When my business was in its infancy, I also made the decision to not travel internationally at all. Long trips can really halt momentum, and I didn't want to interrupt my laser-focus. Since then, James and I have been to over twenty-three countries together. So turn that frown upside down. This is just a season. And it will last as long as it takes for you to get debt-free and build consistent, residual income.

Understanding opportunity cost is crucial to moving forward. Most people struggle deeply with these decisions and choose the "instant gratification" or the "people-pleaser" choice. Most people also turn around in five years and wonder why they aren't any closer to their dreams. Maintaining a daily calendar makes you more aware of the small trade-offs you make every day. Are you diligent with your schedule?

BEING INTENTIONAL DOESN'T REMOVE SPONTANEITY; IT SIMPLY SETS A COURSE FOR CONSISTENT PRODUCTION.

Everyone is busy. There's always something to do, someone to call, an event to respond to. If you say yes to everything and everyone, I can guarantee you will not be hustling smarter anytime soon. There must be priorities.

The HARD decisions are choosing between good and good.

The EASY decisions are saying no to the obvious time wasters.

Here are a few examples of time wasters:

- Watching copious amounts of television.
- Scrolling social media feeds.
- Saying yes to every football game, every party, and every happy hour.
- Floating on the elliptical machine.
- Reading lots of fiction.
- Playing video games or *Candy Crush* nonsense.
- Listening to a morning radio show.

These are just examples of a few time wasters I commonly notice. Do any of these time wasters sound familiar in your own life? None of these activities are *wrong*—but none of them will help you grow. Actually, *Candy Crush* is wrong. No more. Why listen to the radio show on a commute if you could be plugging into an enriching podcast and be inspired for the day? I want you to start thinking this way. Make the best use of your time.

EVERY DAY, YOUR CHOICES WILL LEAD YOU CLOSER TO YOUR DREAMS OR FURTHER AWAY.

Life is too short to trade what you want most for what you want now. And life is definitely too short for Candy Crush.

 REFLECTION SECTION

I want you to pinpoint and destroy time wasters in your life. You are in a hustling season, and you need to create space to crush it on your quest to become a Time Millionaire! What do you need to put aside in this season to free up your bandwidth?

Do you need to:

Turn off *SportsCenter* so next season you can go to any game, any time, sit in any seat, and pay for your best friend too?

Take a break from a volunteering role so you can give more of your time and money than you ever thought possible in three years?

Say no to a birthday party because you already committed to meeting a prospect at that time?

Choose your company's annual convention opposed to going to the family reunion so in two years you can be working from home and quadruple your available hours for family?

Say no to the upcoming getaway with your friends so next year you can take twice as much time off and upgrade to first-class airfare and the suite with view?

Bodybuilding Diaries

By freeing up your "decision-making" bandwidth, it will pave the way for one of the most imperative success ingredients on your journey: the power of FOCUS.

When I was 23 years old, I was inspired to compete in a fitness competition as I was a devoted reader of *Oxygen* magazine and was regularly exposed to the flashy industry. Plus, I figured it could be good for business. I'm all about those #gainz.

Fitness is a category of bodybuilding competitions in which you sculpt your body into a lean, muscular machine—aiming for around 12 percent body fat. You prance around in a bedazzled bikini and five-inch clear stilettos to show off your perfectly balanced curves and perform a two-minute routine that demonstrates your flexibility, strength, and ability to wow the crowd with your stage presence.

Friends and family thought I was off my rocker. People were worried I was getting too bulky. I was antisocial because I had to stay on my tilapia-and-broccoli meal plan and go to bed at 8:30 p.m. every night (did I mention I was 23?!). I turned down date offers, because who wants to go out with someone who has a rigid curfew and has to eat out of Tupperware? Daily, I got confused looks in the weight room as I ran around performing compound moves, such as "burpee-to-squat-jump-to-pull-up," far before exercises like that gained popularity with the HIIT movement. I practiced my routine in the aerobics room at the gym, and I got shy when people stopped to watch as I lip-synced into the mirror while doing a single-arm push-up. My house smelled like asparagus for months. I flared my lats when I walked by mirrors, and I regularly flexed my abs to make sure they were intact. I walked around drinking a milk jug filled with water—#juglife. I worked out twice per day and had to get massages weekly to keep my body loose. I ruined more than one set of sheets with a spray tan that could rival any Oompa Loompa, and just for the heck of it, I decided to go platinum blonde before the show (I was born with jet black hair, so there's that).

I ended up winning first place, and then I retired from the sport because I like food too much.

Although the dieting and wear and tear on my body was arduous, I loved how I felt in that season of competition preparation: fiercely focused. My determination was unwavering. I was calculated with my time and attention. Personal discipline flooded into every area of my life. I love that feeling. I love the results it produces, and the action it evokes. When I am focused, I feel powerful and unstoppable. Decisions are easier because I am nonnegotiable in what I want.

Have you ever seen a big goal come to fruition?

You will recognize the parallel experiences in your own life because you will remember feeling on top of the world for staying true to your goal and pushing yourself beyond what you thought you were capable of.

It is also very possible you have never fully committed to an intimidating goal, and this will be new territory for you. Life just always seems to get in the way. Excuse after excuse, roadblock after roadblock. Either way, it's time to commit to your vision of a preferred future. You *can* do this.

SUCCESS IS SIMPLY A DECISION TO PERSIST WITHOUT EXCEPTION.

To become a Time Millionaire, you must develop unstoppable focus. You must be absolutely ALL-IN on your vision.

> *Life is too short to have one foot in, one foot out.*

 REFLECTION SECTION

Have you worked diligently towards a big goal before? Do you recall fighting for something you believed in, and then relishing in the accomplishment of that dream? Was it worth it?

Chase Your Rabbit

Think what you want about him, but one undeniable truth about Donald Trump is the fact that he is an extremely focused individual who seems to always get what he wants. And it all started with his fixation on the concrete jungle.

Before the reality shows, the books, and the most honorable title in our nation, President Donald J. Trump had the eye of a real estate tycoon tiger. From the early 70's until the early 90's, all he thought about were high rises and casinos and dirt. Match that type of laser focus with an unparalleled work ethic and some serious cajones, and you have a self-made billionaire.

Gary Vaynerchuk is another ballsy entrepreneur who started his journey with one of the world's most ancient commodities: wine. For years and years, he gave absolute attention to the family wine business, helping the company grow from $4 million to over $60 million in sales. Only then did he start to dip his toes into becoming the brash, "say it how it is" personality we see all over social media now. Only then did he become a venture capitalist and step aside from wine to co-found VaynerMedia. Only then.

And how about some others?

- Richard Branson focused on music for 13 years.
- Jeff Bezos focused on books for 4 years.
- Elon Musk focused on software for 6 years.
- Sara Blakely remains focused on spandex; many of us ladies around the globe are indebted to her genius.
- Oprah focused on building her daytime talk show before taking over the world.

Committing to your vision is easy. The hard part is staying focused on it long enough to actually see it through to fruition. Many entrepreneurs are creatives, and we creative-types have idea ADHD. Just ask my husband. His heart skips a beat when I say, "I have an idea!" You must protect yourself from shiny-object syndrome on your quest to #HustleSmarter and fund your dreams.

DISTRACTION IS THE ENEMY OF ACHIEVEMENT.

One of my business mentors always says, "If you chase two rabbits, you'll catch none." He heard it from some guy named Confucius. It basically means that it's hard enough to chase one rabbit, and by trying to chase two, it divides your attention, and therefore it is impossible to achieve #momentumbaby with either.

If you have not fully decided and gone ALL-IN on your vehicle to fund your dreams, you will be forever chasing and never catching. It's exhausting. You must follow *one* course until success. You will find that if you focus on one single business opportunity and excel at it, many other doors will begin to open for you.

Earlier I mentioned how I fell in love with writing when I started my first blog. It was a passion project, but in 2011 when I was living paycheck to paycheck and swamped in thousands of dollars of debt, I shifted my focus to building my direct sales business and completely stopped anything and everything that could distract me from creating #momentumbaby. Bye-bye blog.

Expressing myself with the off chance that it could also entertain, inspire, and/or propel readers into action fed my creative soul, but I had to make a choice. In that season. In that time. When I was living in a studio apartment on Dexter Avenue with sliding glass doors that opened to a freeway. I had to choose.

I had to choose not to do something that mattered to me in order to do what mattered to me MOST.

We are always choosing. Like when I was in that apartment, I chose to believe the sound of cars whizzing by was actually the vibrations of peaceful crashing ocean waves. I nearly convinced myself. I also chose to put writing aside to get my business off the ground. I needed to get free from the shackles of debt, trading dollar for hour, and working grueling long days. I physically could not imagine living that life in my 30's. I had a vision that within five years, I would be debt-free and residual income would allow me to work part-time on my business and full-time on my passion projects. Now here we are.

Steve Jobs once said, "People think focus means saying yes to the thing you've got to focus on. But that's not what it means at all. It means saying no to the hundred other good ideas that there are. You have to pick carefully."

If you have lots of ideas like me, I recommend writing them down and setting them aside for another time. I actually have a Google Doc titled "Angie's Master Plan." It's less scary than it sounds. Essentially, it houses every business idea I've ever thought of. I recognize the timing isn't perfect just yet, but those ideas are there for me when it is the right time. And I will be positioned to fund them myself.

Indecision leads to procrastination, which leads to low self-esteem and lack of action. No action = no results. The more time you wallow in indecision, the longer it will take to get momentum. And as I will touch on in the next chapter: momentum is your BFF as you make significant strides towards any goal.

YOU'LL NEVER KNOW WHO YOU CAN BE AND WHAT YOU CAN DO UNTIL YOU GO ALL-IN.

> *Life is too short to chase two rabbits*
> *and catch neither.*

Now that you have had breakthrough on how you want to live each day, you have acknowledged the goals you want to achieve and you recognize the undeniable focus required to reach them, it's time to get specific on the "how-to's" of building the ultimate side hustle.

CHAPTER 6

_____

BUILD YOUR BUSINESS ON A SOLID FOUNDATION

It's Not How. It's Who.

"Hey, girl. So I'm thinking about pursuing this business, and there's an event 20 minutes from you tonight. I really think it's up your alley, and you should check it out. Interested?"

Little did I know that five seconds of courage to call my longtime girlfriend, Stephanie, would result in huge blessings for both of our families. Stephsta is a high-income earner on our team, and because she opened her heart and got to work in 2012, she is now a full-time mompreneur, working from home while raising her two beautiful children.

So here you are: You've mapped out your goals. You've chosen a company that aligns with your values. You love the products, the people, and the potential for income. You're fired up, ready to go. Now what? You go to your coach and ask, "How do I start making money?" A great coach will not respond with *how*. They will ask...*who*?

THIS IS A "WHO DO YOU KNOW" BUSINESS.

Who is in your "warm market" that could benefit from what you have your hands on?

Your warm market are people you know on a first-name basis, such as coworkers, friends from the gym, friends from school, etc. At first, it's common to be nervous about sharing with them. After all, you are brand new at this, and unless you have spent days reading every document on your company's website, you likely don't know a whole lot of details outside of the fact that you're pumped up and have a vision for how your products and opportunity can make a difference for people. But slight nervousness is not only common, it's good. You need to recognize the power of getting uncomfortable, and it starts now.

To avoid this common fear, new distributors will often get the bright idea to start with their "cold market." Meaning people they don't have a previous relationship with such as a grocery store clerk, an Uber driver, or the shop owner down the street. Out of sheer velocity and numbers, you may have nominal success with this at best. When you don't have a track record with someone, it can often take much longer to build enough trust for them to listen to you, so your likeliness of success is lower, potentially leaving you discouraged very quickly.

In the first week of starting my business, I shared the opportunity with two people who were open to it. The first was Stephanie, in my warm market, who I mentioned above. The second person who didn't completely turn me down was a local gym owner of whom I had no previous track record. I blindly walked into his studio, asked if he had a nutrition program for his clients, and if he was open to an additional income stream. He did not say yes right away, but he did say yes to an appointment, which is a huge win. I introduced him to my mentor, and he dabbled with the business for several years. In the end, he had "lone ranger" syndrome; he was not responsive to coaching and ended up drifting off.

As long as you haven't been an unreliable jerk to your friends and family, you will have the most success with them to begin with. Start by making a list of every single person you can think of who could benefit from your products and/or extra income. Even if you aren't sure how they will respond, if they come to mind, write their name down. And write down people who just plain like you. They may be the biggest cheerleaders in your new venture. Go through your phone contacts, your Facebook friends, and your email database. Think about past and current coworkers, parents of your kids' friends, and high school buddies. Don't pre-judge or rule anyone out. Let them decide if it is for them or not.

We have all been exposed to relationships through a variety of networks in our lives. My first several years were dominated by my contacts in pageants, the Greek system, and the gym I worked at. Truthfully, you will have faster results in this business from the get-go if you have made a conscious effort in your life to be a positive, involved, connected person. But if you haven't, don't rule yourself out. The average person still knows 200 people! I have witnessed people with next to zero influence and very few quality relationships grow their business to monumental levels through an unwavering commitment to the process.

To be sure, not everyone will say yes. In fact, most won't. If you are getting one yes for every ten people you talk to, you're doing great. This is a numbers game and large numbers will prevail. Keep your head up and remember that no often means "not right now." There will be skeptics, and some people annoyingly will just not respond at all. I promise that this happens to everyone. As you stay the course, you will become more attractive by gaining confidence, fine-tuning your message, and remaining consistent, which will allow you to draw attention later on from some who said no initially.

You cannot do this business without a list! At every stage in this business, you must work from a list.

 REFLECTION SECTION

Develop your warm market list. Who do you know that could benefit from your products? Who do you know that may want to become a Time Millionaire with you? Who do you know that simply loves you and wants to support you? Go through your phone and social media contacts. Write their names down. This is your working capital.

Filling Your Pipeline

As you build momentum with your warm market by helping a handful of customers get results, you will start to generate more referrals. This will be a ginormous part of your business, and it is why it's absolutely critical you treat your business as a professional from day one, offering stellar customer service and impeccable reliability.

If you want to move faster, it is also wise to have a plan in place to continue generating leads and "fill your pipeline." Often you will share with people and the timing may not be right for them to get started. This is a seed planted, and when there are many seeds planted, there is an inevitable harvest season that will come. No seeds, no harvest. You must always be planting and nurturing for future business. So how can you plant more seeds? You meet more people. At all times, I commit to at least three sources for meeting new people.

Here are a few ideas for places to meet prospects:

- Fitness classes
- Rotary club
- Chamber of Commerce
- Toastmasters
- Meetup.com
- Volunteer organizations
- Recreational sports
- Mom groups
- Church
- Booths at fairs or events
- Business networking (BNI, LeTip, etc.)
- Kid's school and sports

Some of these require a financial investment on your part, while others do not. Simply make a wise decision based on where you are at and where you want to go. I recommend trying a group out, and if it feels like the "right" crowd, commit for a minimum of 90 days to build relationships and make progress. Understand that there's no way to know for sure if something is going to be worth your time. Part of the entrepreneurial journey is working hard and smart and having faith that the right people will be brought to you.

One of my mentors attended a 7 a.m. networking group before he went to his full-time 9-to-5 job every Friday for five years. It was exhausting, inconvenient, and required serious commitment. Would it be worth it? He often wondered. Years down the road, a hairstylist he had met in this group and who had been ordering the product called him up and said she was ready to build the business. She and her husband went on to become some of the fastest growing distributors the company has ever seen.

Worth it? A million times over, he will tell you.

There is no shortcut in this business. It is about building relationships with people, and that cannot be microwaved. Always work from a list. Always have ongoing resources to meet new prospects. Always do the hard stuff even when you don't feel like it.

> *Life is too short to waste time looking*
> *for a shortcut.*

REFLECTION SECTION

What are three new sources you can commit to? Do a little research and implement your involvement immediately.

... If You Do Want a Shortcut ...

If there ever was a "secret" to how people build a business quickly, #momentumbaby would be it. When you have momentum, it makes you look better than you actually are, and when you don't have momentum, you look worse than you actually are.

MOMENTUM MAKES BIG THINGS SMALL AND IMPOSSIBLE THINGS POSSIBLE.

Momentum does not mean win after win after win; it means there is a force that is moving forward in an unstoppable manner that creates more and more energy as it continues to plummet in a positive, focused direction. Momentum is your new best friend, and you must do everything in your power to create it and keep it.

How to Create #MOMENTUMBABY

Creating momentum requires both the work of the heart (mass) and the work of the hands (velocity).

Momentum = Mass x Velocity

The workings of the heart—or mass—are the intangibles of your business. They include your beliefs, attitude, integrity, teachability, commitment to grow, core values, focus, thoughts, and so on. I will be going into much more detail on these intangibles in the final chapter.

The workings of the hands—or velocity—are the tangibles of your business. They include daily action, discipline, follow-up, being organized, consistency, showing up to events, coaching your team, and so on.

WHEN YOU ARE EQUALLY TAKING MASSIVE ACTION AND GROWING PERSONALLY, YOU CREATE #MOMENTUMBABY.

Momentum Killers

Essentially anything that distracts you from keeping the main thing the main thing, or displays a lack of consistency to your team, will halt momentum and must be avoided in your early stages of business growth.

Here are a few examples:
- Extended travel (3 or more weeks)
- "Checking out" for a few months
- Getting lazy with follow-up
- Missing local and major events
- Starting another business
- Dysfunction in your family life
- Moving out of the area

Don't ignore the beautiful power of #momentumbaby. Do what ever it takes to keep it and sustain it as you work to become a Time Millionaire.

 REFLECTION SECTION

Given your history, which of these momentum killers might you commonly face? How can you plan ahead now to overcome any distractions?

Getting Over FOWOT

Leading a volunteer army, I witness people backing out on their word and dreams quite often. Sometimes it's not the right timing or the right fit, but most times, it's because of FOWOT: Fear Of What Others Think.

At some sort of level, nearly every one of us worries about what other people think. Our desire to be socially validated by others is engrained in our DNA. It can be totally crippling, and working through this block can mean the difference between a mediocre life with regrets in our last days, or a crazy, ridiculous, awesome, extraordinary life with nothing but joy when we bid farewell to this world. Sounds heavy, but it's the truth. Admitting your mortality will give you the boldness to pursue your purpose with urgency. It's time you no longer live at the mercy of biased perspectives.

So how does one overcome FOWOT?

First, you need to ask yourself: "What do I believe about me?"

What we believe about ourselves deep down is what comes out in our actions. We can never consistently perform at a level that is inconsistent with how we see ourselves.

For example, if underneath the layers you do not believe you have what it takes to be an entrepreneur, you will likely crumble at the first sign of adversity. You will start believing your own excuses and what your mom said about "how most businesses fail and you better have a backup plan!" You'll start tuning into the negative forces instead of the desires of your heart. Everyone else's opinion will matter so much to you, even though everyone else doesn't pay your bills and doesn't share your dreams, and frankly doesn't care that much about your future happiness.

But if at your core you believe you do have what it takes to be an entrepreneur—even though it doesn't make sense on paper and you have yet to develop many skills—you will start tuning out the endless opinions of everyone else. You will begin to take small steps in the right direction. You will become who you need to become to get the job done. And as you continue to march forward in faith, you will uncover more and more competence and confidence through repetition. And as you grow in competence and confidence, you will become more attractive, sending a powerful message to the world. The world will take notice, and even more people will line up to follow your vision.

You know the desires of your heart, now you must accept that not everyone will understand your motives. Hear me now:

There's no shame in going after your dreams as long as you are acting with love and integrity. We all have access to joy and freedom, but nothing will steal from you faster than FOWOT.

Your thoughts and beliefs about yourself are so deeply rooted that it may take time to transform your beliefs to be in alignment with the life you want. So here's another question I want you to write down: "Who *am* I?"

Sit in stillness and ask yourself this question. Let go of who you think you should be to society, your family, and so on. Ask who you are. And most importantly, once you have the answer, BELIEVE IT. Call it in. Repeat it. Walk in it. You are beautifully and wonderfully made. The world needs you to say yes to your true self. The more I believe what my heavenly Father says about me and the less I seek validation from the world, the freer I am. Every one of us was born with the birthright of *choice*.

It's not your job to win everyone's approval. Your job is to attend to the dream planted in your soul.

> *Life is too short to be bound by the opinions of others.*

 REFLECTION SECTION

"What do I believe about me?"..."Who am I?"...

You Can Do Hard Things

Finding freedom from the opinions of others is hard, no doubt about it. But nothing about this journey to become a Time Millionaire is easy. Stop chasing easy; start chasing the life you deeply, truly want. Besides, you *can* do hard things.

In 2005, I arrived in Seattle licking my wounds after getting rejected by USC, Pepperdine, *and* UCLA. I had accepted my fate as a Husky, and I was bright-eyed and hopeful for this new season as a freshman at the University of Washington (UW). I wasn't particularly excited about the prospect of sharing a Victorian mansion with 100 other girls, but more than a few people had told me that the Greek system was a fantastic tool for networking, and I had heard enough times in my life, "It's not *what* you know—it's *who* you know," so I decided to give sorority life a try.

Rushing at UW is a 5-day process of putting your best face forward; mingling, and interviewing with ladies at each of the sixteen houses. At the end of every day, you rate the houses you connect with, and they rate you back. If the interest is mutual, you get invited back for another round of interviews.

I thought it was going to be a breeze. I was a pageant girl after all. Who wouldn't want a pageant girl? My community service track record was supreme, and I could pull off a crop top with ease. I would simply choose my favorite house, and they would choose me back. They would welcome me with loving arms and pull me into their sisterhood of pillow fights, sharing lip gloss, and gossiping about frat boys.

The first day came and went, and when I woke up the next morning to see who invited me back, none of my top houses were on the list. Stamped with rejection. I took a deep breath and reminded myself there were plenty of more houses I could fit into. I put on another perfectly orchestrated outfit and headed out for round two. Once again, I was not invited back to any of my top choices. Rejected. Again. I saw the next four years of my life flash before my eyes in a house that didn't suit my style. What if I got put in the frumpy-girl house?! I was a bit chubby from discovering Mike's Hard Lemonade over summer break. Maybe that was it. My ego was being threatened in an entirely new way.

Another day came and went, and more rejection with it. I was bewildered and crushed. But that little voice that helps me make decisions whispered, "It will all work out. Stick with it." Finally, decision day came, and I was chosen by a house that was never even on my radar, but I felt relieved to have even been accepted at all. I believed in that voice. I believed it would end well. And I'm glad I listened.

At least a third of my *entire* business has been generated from fellow sisters I met within my sorority and the relationships I built throughout the entire Greek system. Not only was it an incredible blessing for my personal training business early on, but I have also now worked with dozens of sisters on their health goals through my nutrition coaching business as well. In fact, one particular meeting at a Starbucks resulted in enormous impact for everyone involved.

It was early 2012, and I was still fresh into my network marketing business. I met with a fellow PC (pledge class) from

2005 and designed a program for her nutrition and fitness goals. By this point, I had also learned to ask, "Are you interested in the opportunity to earn some extra income as well?" She said no but said her mom might be interested. A few weeks later, I got connected with her mom, who was in the thick of aiding her ill father, so the timing wasn't right. She would contact me when it was, though. I followed up every few months, and one year later, she was ready. I began coaching her on the business, and one of the first people she introduced me to was her neighbor, who went on to lose more than fifty pounds and caught a glimpse of the opportunity. The neighbor shared with her best friend's dad, and as he was desperate to get healthy, he got started on our top nutritional jumpstart program. He also went on to get in the best shape of his life. I asked him, "Who do you know that may be interested in this opportunity?" He eventually introduced me to his daughter, and she was the one who really took to the business with a long-term vision and became one of the top leaders on our team. Tremendous impact that would have never existed had I given up during rush week!

Building a freedom-based lifestyle is not going to be easy. Nothing worthwhile is easy. But here is the good news: You can do hard things. Seriously, if I can survive the soul-crushing realities of sorority rush week, you can build a network marketing business.

STOP RUNNING FROM HARD THINGS.
YOU ARE NOT A QUITTER.

There is a plan and purpose for your life even bigger than you can imagine, but because it is so big, so is the attack. Everything that comes against your destiny is an attack. There is a force in this world that doesn't want you to succeed. Most people fail at chasing their dreams because this force downloads into them excuse after excuse when steps are taken in a positive direction. This force tries to numb you with distractions and lure you into complacency. There are battles you must watch out for along your journey. I've identified them below so you can be aware when they try to derail you even in the slightest of ways.

8 Battles Every Distributor Faces

1. Uncertainty: Some people never fully allow themselves to go all-in with network marketing because they want to be certain it is the right business model, the right company, the right product, and the right timing. But they are ignoring one simple reality: nothing is certain. Jobs aren't certain. Promotions aren't certain. The housing market isn't certain. Political systems aren't certain. Currencies aren't certain. "What if it doesn't work?" they worry. Ironically, their current plan is already not working, and that is why they need another vehicle for income.

2. Fear of exposure: Living in fear of what other people think is so common I devoted an entire section to it earlier in this chapter. I'll just leave you with one more thought on the matter: nobody else is paying your bills. And in 100 years, we will all be in the dirt, and none of this FOWOT nonsense will matter.

3. Fear of failure: Fear of failure is my personal biggest battle. When investing time and trying something new, I have to continually remind myself that failure is part of the learning process. I feel this fear creep in especially after I have already had nominal success under my belt. There is more pressure to succeed, or at least I convince myself there is because people are watching and expect me to succeed. One practice that helps me combat this fear is to focus on my daily tasks and not to get lost down a road of preemptive what-ifs. I have goals with dates attached, but if I don't reach them in time, I have a committee meeting with myself to ask what I could be doing better. I then make small changes and keep marching forward, extending the timeline of the goal.

4. Fear of success: This fear is the concept that we are scared of achieving what we want to achieve. The most common reason people fear success is because they fear the change and responsibility that will accompany the newfound success. It often prompts questions about whether you can live up to people's new expectations of you, or if you even want to have to do that. Just like fear of failure, there is no magic formula for overcoming this. It starts by becoming aware of whether you are self-sabotaging your efforts and then consciously choosing not to do so.

5. Fear of no help: When things aren't going their way, people like to find things to complain about, and one of those complaints is commonly, "I don't like my sponsor! They never help me." I can't speak for every MLM organization, but I know within ours there is *always* help upline if you ask. Most people just don't ask.

Make it a point to immediately go up your lineage until you find the upline leader who has displayed longevity and proven results for their team. Introduce yourself, and do whatever it takes to spend time with them and learn from them. I am fortunate in that the couple who is my direct upline sponsor is one of the top-earning distributorships in the company. If you are still choosing a company to align with, do your best to sign up with a distributor who has vision and success under their belt.

6. People quitting on you: Of course it stings when someone cries on your shoulder telling you they are ready for change and the next thing you know they haven't returned your last five calls. Or texts. Or emails. Or pokes on Facebook. JK, too far, too far. I call it "going dark." It's even harder if they've worked with you for several years and they get distracted with life or lose their belief and decide to retreat back to old ways. "People are a mystery," my mentor always says. This is a tough reality for this business because you are working with a volunteer army. I've never met a single high-income earner that this hasn't happened to countless times.

7. Personal attacks: Friends, family, and/or Facebook trolls will likely attack at unpredictable moments. Whether it's a snarky remark about the products you distribute or a general skepticism in the MLM business model, the attacks will come because people fear what they don't know. You can't take it personally. Shed a tear, and move on.

8. Time management: Many people talk themselves out of building freedom with direct sales because they are "too busy." The reality is that everyone is too busy. When you already have a full plate of commitments but you want to be a Time Millionaire, you will have to eliminate some things. You must become a person of your word and get to places on time. People who are successful in this business simply make it a priority. And it's worth it. I truly believe you can do more with this vehicle in 2 years than you can with 20 years in Corporate America. Learn how to prioritize, time block, and say yes and no when it matters.

Can you identify a pattern in yourself? Of quitting? Getting sidetracked or distracted? Wanting to "check out"? You can no longer be captive by your past. Instead, you must be captivated by your purpose.

Have you used any of these excuses lately?

"I don't have enough time."

"I don't have enough money."

"I'm not as talented as that person."

"My genetics make it harder."

"I'm too old."

"I'm too young."

"I'm not that type of person."

"I'm not good at that."

"My friends will think I'm nuts."

"I'm not qualified enough."

ENOUGH! Draw the line and decide.

THE REASONS WE SAY WE CAN'T DO SOMETHING ARE THE REASONS WE SHOULD DO THAT THING.

> *Life is too short to let your purpose become your excuse.*

The Hardest Part

I've been self-employed since I was 21 years old. It's all I know. So when I committed to my direct sales business in 2011, it wasn't a novel idea to go out and drum up prospects. Although it's extremely difficult to pinpoint an exact number, most sources estimate only 10 to 15 percent of Americans own a business. That leaves nearly 85 percent who may be completely new to entrepreneurship when they get started with network marketing.

THE HARDEST PART ABOUT THIS BUSINESS IS THAT YOU WILL NEVER HAVE A BOSS AND YOU CAN NEVER GET FIRED.

This sounds kind of perfect, right? Well, not quite. Hear me out. When you don't have a boss and you can never get fired—and you have a full-time income from your job so you're getting by OK—it can be very tempting to slack off. Not only do you need to learn how to employ yourself, but you also must create a sense of urgency to see it through. Even now, I have to continually motivate myself to do what needs to get done when nobody is watching. Let me give you some pointers on doing just that.

How to Employ Yourself

1. Be relentless with your schedule: If you have been sloppy with your schedule in the past, you must adopt a new way of time management and corresponding habits immediately. I mentioned time-blocking in the previous section, but let's get deeper into this because it is such a hang-up for many. I suggest blocking specific time every Sunday, say 3 to 4 p.m., to map out your entire week. Set aside 8 hours for sleep and the rest of the time should be filled with the following: reading, working out, fulfilling your day-job requirements, contributing to church and/or community activities, having family time, and building your business. Occasionally there will be social events trickled in, but be very careful what you say yes and no to. Third cousin's second birthday parties can quickly take over your discretionary time and steal you from making progress on your business plan.

2. Focus on income-producing activities: With the time you do dedicate to your business, be sure you are doing activities that move the ball down the field. Nearly 90 percent of your efforts should be focused on talking to people. This includes following up with customers, sharing your story with new prospects, networking online and in-person, introducing prospects to your sponsor, and/

or inviting to events. And again. And again. And again and again. Always work from a list, and meet people at their interest level. Some may only be interested in your products—that's great! Give them results by offering excellent customer service, and be sure to ask for referrals. Some may be intrigued by the Time Millionaire lifestyle and start asking you questions about the opportunity. Share your story with strength, and show them what's impossible. When you get your first "YES!" on the business, congrats! Now you have a team to coach as well. Focus on serving people and your business will grow.

3. Create a sense of urgency: Raising necessity is your antidote to procrastination. Have you ever met someone who has gone through a traumatic accident? Perhaps a severe car wreck? Or they survived cancer at a young age? One thing I've noticed about these champions is they live with a healthy respect for the shortness of life. They live with urgency and intention. When something doesn't serve their mission, they aren't afraid to say, "I ain't got time for dat!" Even if you've never gone through something life-threatening yourself, you will need to raise necessity behind the time you spend on your business. Having very clear goals, timelines attached to those goals, and consequences for not reaching those goals within the timelines will prompt you to take action even when you feel it would be easy to put it off until tomorrow.

4. Stay connected to the mother ship: In the beginning stages of your business, you should be talking to your mentor every single day. They are there to walk you through the highs and lows.

They are there for support—and tough love. Talk to them about specific conversations you are having. Ask for word choices about exact scenarios. Discuss objections you have been getting and how to respond. Also, if you are in a region with high-income earners who regularly host events, don't you dare miss even one. Make them a high priority. Events are your chance to continue learning as well as your chance to show prospects the big picture. If you are not in a region with established leadership, you will need to plant the flag. Ask your mentor how you should go about organizing your first event.

In general, those who treat their network marketing business like a job get rewarded handsomely.

Would you show up late to your job? Would you ignore due dates? Or take several days to respond to your boss? Would you scroll Facebook while on the clock? Would you take 10 weeks off per year? Hopefully not. And the same integrity and effort should be applied to your business.

Learnable Skills

Network marketing is an even playing field for any personality type and any background. You do not have to be the life of the party or display infectious charisma. You do, however, need to develop skills in order to go far. The great news is that these skills can be taught and learned by anyone with a heart for growth.

Here are the top four skills you need to adopt as quickly as possible:

1. Invite with Strength

By setting an appointment with someone—or getting someone to an event—I have achieved the crucial first step in doing business together. For me, it is a win if I can simply get them to hear about my products and opportunity. At that point, it is up to them to walk through the open door and for me to do the proper follow up.

With your phone call, you are interrupting people's daily programming because you believe you have your hands on something that could change their lives. But it won't be easy. You are competing with their busy schedule—or worse, the latest season of *Stranger Things*. To pull them away from their couch and convince them to drive through traffic after a full workday, you must have a compelling invitation by speaking directly to what's in it for them. People don't generally care about how much you love it and what it's going to do for you—they want to know why *they* will love it and what it will do for *them*! Why they can't live without it. Why missing out on it will hurt them. To get this message across, you need to develop the skill of inviting with strength.

Here are some tips on how to be a pro at inviting:

A) Do it in-person or over the phone. NO texts or emails unless you have exhausted all other efforts. It is more powerful if someone can hear the tone and conviction in your voice.

B) Make it personal. Your prospect is tuned into the radio channel called, "What's in it for me?" Speak specifically to what they have expressed needing a solution to. Recently, James and I went on a dinner date with another couple. They have a baby on the way, and the husband shared the concern that the career path he chose isn't exactly lucrative, and keeping up with the rising cost of living has become a huge area of stress. James called him later and said, "I'm calling because the last few times we've talked, you've mentioned you feel trapped by your earning potential. Are you open to hearing about what Angie and I do to help people build a secondary income?" So simple.

C) Be authentic. Don't be flighty or dance around the subject. Get straight to the point by starting with something like, "Do you have a minute? There's something coming up I want to invite you to." And by all means, say the name of your company and be completely honest about why you're calling. Shadiness will get you nowhere.

Invite according to their personality type. If you know your prospect well enough, you can tune into the "What's in it for me?" station even deeper by speaking directly to what motivates their personality type using the DISC method (https://www.123test.com/disc-personality-test/). I encourage you to take the test yourself if you haven't already, and then read more extensively on each type. Below is an extremely brief explanation of each type:

- **Dominance.** D's are results-oriented and are motivated by challenges. They hate small talk or beating around the bush. I'm a D, so the best way to get me somewhere is to tell me it will save me time, and I will walk away knowing if it is for me or not.

- **Influence.** I's thrive off collaboration and building relationships. They hate being ignored. Invite I's by emphasizing community and how fun it's going to be ... there's even going to be a raffle!
- **Steadiness.** S's like to cooperate and are very sincere. They hate being rushed. Invite S's by telling them it would mean a lot if they gave you support by showing up.
- **Conscientiousness.** C's are highly concerned with quality and accuracy. They fear being wrong or missing the mark. Invite C's by telling them they will get all the facts needed to make an educated decision.

2. Become a Storyteller

Storytelling is arguably the most powerful tool in your selling toolbox. Stories help clarify your message and give an instant understanding of the benefits someone gets by working with you. Stories build trust, motivate people to take action, and bring emotion to facts. With the inundation of advertising messages and noise in the marketplace, stories are the fastest and most effective way to grab someone's attention.

The essence of storytelling involves you walking someone through a painful problem either you or someone who has benefitted from your product have overcome. Describe how you solved the problem and achieved the result this prospect is looking for. When I am speaking to someone who wants to lose fifty pounds, I don't dwell on my personal story of how I gained ten pounds of muscle on our products. Instead, I pull out a story of someone like my girlfriend, Liz, who I have helped reclaim her health and life by losing seventy pounds.

Stories sell and facts tell. Make sure you are rooted in your own personal story, and also have a handful of success stories in your back pocket that you are confident sharing at any given time.

3. Ask Questions

It truly astounds me how lost the art of connection is in our world of the wild wild interwebs. I can pretty much guarantee that if you master the art of question asking, you will break many awkward silences and become very likable in your lifetime. This skill is actually quite simple: lead every conversation you engage in by listening 90 percent of the time and responding only 10 percent of the time. Simple, but not easy, because most of us loooove hearing the sound of our own voices. But by controlling yourself and continually putting the ball in the court of this potential prospect, it allows you to find an open door to share your story.

Until this becomes second nature for you, physically write out ten go-to questions you can start any conversation with. Here are a few of my go-to questions:

"Where do you live? Do you enjoy living there?"

"What is your family life like? Married? Single?"

"What do you do for work? Do you love your job?"

"What do you do in your spare time?"

"What are you most excited about in life right now?"

4. Cast a Vision

Great leaders HAVE vision and CAST vision. First, let's focus on having vision. You must get clear on **your personal** vision, which is what Chapters 1 and 5 of this book are dedicated to. Next, you need a **team vision**. This involves getting into the heart of other people's dreams. I even created a mission statement for my own team: "Our mission is to free people of poor health, self-doubt, and financial strife." I can tell you the drive and purpose behind every distributor in our organization. Their purpose becomes my purpose. Finally, you need a **corporate vision**. This will be a direct reflection of the entire company. It includes where you fit in and how you will contribute to the bigger mission.

The next step is to master the ability to cast vision for other people. Through asking the right questions to get to the root of what makes them tick, you can then pull out dreams that have likely been stuffed deep down for years because of fear and doubt. The right questions to ask will require boldness and depth. You become great by unlocking the emotional cord of what is ailing them and courageously painting a picture of what could be by working with you.

Gather people, lead with stories, engage with questions, share a vision of what is possible, and you will be well on your way to growing a massive organization.

> *Life is too short to convince yourself you don't have what it takes when in reality it is completely your choice to master these skills or not.*

Commit to the Process

Laying in a knitted hammock, the warm afternoon breeze swinging me back and forth, my Kindle resting on my chest and my eyes gazing at the grass hut ceiling above me, I felt overcome with gratitude. Then I saw a cockroach dart across the patio, and I remembered I should take a shower.

The day before, after eight hours of flying across the entire country, James and I had landed in the far northeast corner of Brazil and headed west on an exhilarating (read: terrifying) 4-hour road trip. Donkeys walking on the medians. People riding bikes with friends on their handlebars on the freeway in no distinct lanes. Reggae music bouncing across the buildings. Families convening on their front steps and surveying us closely as we drove by. And, there were speed bumps *everywhere*. And I mean everywhere. With no warning. No signs. No lights. Just bumps. Big ones. Wide ones. Short ones. High ones.

Like most husbands, James seems to enjoy evoking me with his driving. It took him a handful of speed bumps before he backed down and took the pedal off the metal. About an hour outside of town, we finally got into a good driving groove and were treated by the most ginormous full orangey moon I have ever seen. Occasionally, we passed pick-up trucks full of people riding in the back and wondered where they could possibly be going. This road seemed to lead to nowhere.

With hours to go and nothing but darkness ahead, I got bored with the nonexistent cell service and asked James, "Truth or truth?" Kind of like truth or dare but a car game, so no dares. I couldn't think of a single question to ask him I didn't already know, so I changed the subject and asked him what he wanted to name our future kids. "I like Luciana and Alessandra." *How very Italian of you, hunny.* I was about to respond when I looked ahead a few feet and screamed "SPEED BUMP!!!!!!!!" He was going 60 mph, and we straight nailed it, *Dukes of Hazzard-style.* The biggest speed bump I had ever seen. We landed after ample air time. The car seemed to be in one piece still. We had all of our limbs. *Phew.*

Both of us were on the edge of our seats with our eyes glued to the road in anticipation of another ambush. Eventually, we pulled in to a town called Barreirinhas. With dirt roads and groups of men hanging in packs at every turn, it was raw and eerie. At long last, we pulled into our *pousada,* relieved to find a nice room with AC. I asked James to check the room for insects. I was at my wit's end. He promised me no bugs.

Getting to Lençóis Maranhenses National Park was, well, no walk in the park. I was adamant that we should skip it all together and stay put in the posh beach town of Armação dos Búzios for the remainder of our time in Brazil, but James was unwavering. He was convinced we would witness true natural wonder. And he was right. It was the most beautiful place I had ever seen with my own two eyes. It was composed of immense, white, sweeping sand dunes with pockets of crystal clear lagoons. These freshwater lakes form during the rainy season. They are warm, clean, and virtually untouched. It was a playground for adventure and beauty. A truly unique travel experience. "And to think, you fought this kicking and screaming." Of course, it's the husband's job to remind you he was right. I consented. The inconvenience to get there was so worth it.

Whether it's laying your eyes on unspoiled natural wonders, achieving monumental changes in your health and fitness, creating a marriage of love and trust, or building your freedom-based business—fulfilling dreams requires you to commit to a process. This process is often much *different, harder,* and *longer* than you originally expected. But you must persist without exception, because the result is often even better than you originally imagined as well.

At times, the temptation to quit will be so incredibly strong as one of the main battles we face in life is discouragement. Discouragement can easily knock you off your feet and make you question whether you should be giving up on your business — wondering whether achieving your dream is even possible. When this happens I want you to remember: You are not alone.

One of the best ways to be encouraged is through community. Find like-minded entrepreneurs to connect with. Share struggles, triumphs, and laugh together. I have a few "crossline" buddies in my inner circle I can lean my head on in times of distress. (Crossline refers to other distributors within my company who are not in my upline or downline.) I also remain encouraged by feeding my soul with enriching books and podcasts. I recommend picking up _Time Millionaire_ any time you are feeling deflated. Lastly, always go back to your WHY. Your why, or purpose, is the reason you are building this business. It's the reason you absolutely must obtain time and financial freedom. Stay hopeful, be unwavering, and get into action.

THE KEY TO YOUR BETTER FUTURE IS TO COMMIT TO THE PROCESS.

Decide. Commit. Act.

> *Life is too short to quit.*
> *Unless you are talking about your job ...*

When to Call it Quits

Leaving the comfort of a secure paycheck can be terrifying. Not only do you say goodbye to the salary but all the perks as well. Health insurance, company car allowances, and expense accounts. A clear and respectable path. It's what you've always known, and there is a degree of comfort and security you feel with it.

But you know what's not terrifying? Waking up whenever you decide to start your day. Never asking permission for vacation time. Traveling for epic experiences instead of hopping a plane to Missoula, Montana for a two-hour meeting. Being excited when the phone buzzes opposed to being nervous that it could be your boss micromanaging your every move. Being available for a friend in need. Sitting in the stands at every game cheering on your kiddos.

I'll never forget the day I officially "retired" from personal training. It was an odd feeling to be leaving my clients by choice; clients I had grown to know and love. Clients I worked very hard to obtain and retain. Clients who supported and encouraged me through the many ups and downs I faced as a spandex entrepreneur in my early 20's. But I was sick and tired of missing dinner with James. I was sick and tired of having zero energy to create. For 18 months, I had been hustling smarter to get free, and it was time to take the leap.

I trained my last client on a Monday and then boarded a plane to London. It was Christmas Eve 2012. It was a big day. I left the only career I'd ever known and lost my international business class virginity all in one day. James and I laid our seats flat and had way too much fun delighting in our five-course dinner while strategically pressing play on our touch screens to watch movies in sync.

Little did I know that in just a few short hours Jamesy would be kneeling on the bank of the Thames River, with the London Eye as our backdrop, asking me the question I had been longing to hear since the moment I met him on his magic carpet on that hot summer night under a madrona tree. Little did I know we would celebrate by giving double high-fives to the homeless in the park and making out as the rain started pouring down before hopping in our Range Rover back to the Andaz. Little did I know the magic in store for us.

We continued our engagement escapades through Spain and Portugal, but I was attacked viciously with fear throughout that trip. Had I left my clients too soon? What if my direct sales business stopped working for me? What if my success was a fluke? What if, what if!?!

Fear is such a buzzkill. And it is rarely accurate. My business had so much momentum when I returned from those three weeks abroad, my paychecks started doubling, resulting in my first six-figure year in 2013. My life was never the same again.

In 2014, James and I attended a conference for our company. He was so inspired by the stories he heard, he decided to leave his real estate job and join me. But it was far too soon. We were still in debt to Uncle Sam. Even though we were earning a six-figure income with the business, the cost of living in Seattle was rising at an alarming rate. Making $250,000 per year had become the new $100,000 up in our pocket of the world. I had been the driver in the business up until this point, and he wasn't sure how to step into it without ever personally laying the groundwork himself. It created enormous stress to lose his income, and we were a hot mess for nine months trying to figure it all out. By 2015, he had created opportunity in real estate again, and we felt like ourselves to have dual income, grateful to have made it through that season.

In my experience, most people leave their job too early. It's a delicate balance to be sure, but here is the formula that worked for me and what I recommend:

1. Start by building your direct sales business in the hours between your full-time job.
2. Use the extra income to pay off any debt with speed.
3. Once debt-free and earning *twice* as much with your business as your full-time job, consider leaving your job to put more effort into growing your network marketing business and building your freedom-based lifestyle.

The bottom line is that you need cash flow to invest back into your business, and running an organization out of desperation is highly unattractive. Be patient with the plan, and when the timing is right, make the jump into your freedom-based lifestyle.

Life is too short to build someone else's dream.

You've been forming your vision, belief and confidence. You're clear on the direct sales business model and why it is the ultimate side hustle. You understand the basic skills and mindset required to get your business up and running. Now, let's tie it all together with the most important element to business success: personal success.

CHAPTER 7

PERSONAL GROWTH FAST TRACK

Attracting Winners

When I first started out in my business, my mentor engrained this thought into me: "Your business grows as YOU personally grow!" OK. Cool. Got it. Except, what do you *mean* by personal growth? One thing I knew for sure was that I wanted my business to grow. I was hungry and determined, so I had to figure out what it means to personally grow. And quickly.

Read self-help, leadership, and mindset books? Check. Surround myself with encouraging people? Check. Show up on time? Check. Offer excellent customer service? Check. Work diligently and do what I say I'm going to do? Check, and check.

But what else could I do to fast track my growth...?

Here is what I discovered: growing personally is waking up every day and asking, "What is getting in the way of who I am now and who I want to become? Is it a way of thinking? A habit? My activity?" The beginning place of growth is to define reality. Once you identify what is holding you back, the transformation will happen when you choose to make a change and overcome whatever is between you and the best version of you.

YOU DON'T HAVE TO BE PERFECT; YOU HAVE TO BE WILLING TO GROW.

My biggest motivator for going on a trip around the world aside from watching Sweet Jamesy fulfill a lifelong dream was that I knew I couldn't possibly do something completely out of routine and not grow personally in a big way. The interesting thing is I didn't notice a ton of growth while traveling. I still felt enslaved by impatience and a need for control. But three, six, eight months down the road upon our return, I began to see incredible shifts in the way I thought and how I treated people. I started living in full surrender. I literally felt like I had zipped off a bad costume I had been wearing for so many years, keeping me tethered to a false identity, and walked into a new me. The me I was created to be.

TO THE DEGREE WE ARE TRANSFORMED, THE WORLD IS TRANSFORMED.

Becoming a Time Millionaire requires you to become a leader. You must remain fresh on the inside if you desire to lead others to victory in their lives. You must constantly self-reflect in stillness and ask, "What is holding me back from becoming the me I was created to be?" You must overcome fear and laziness—the main culprits standing between you and your dreams. By doing so, you will attract the type of people you dream about doing business and life with, and you will be prepared to lead.

WE DON'T ATTRACT WHAT WE NEED OR WANT, WE ATTRACT WHAT WE BECOME.

Who are you becoming?

> *Life is too short to not become the best version of you.*

 REFLECTION SECTION

What is holding you back from being the BEST version of you?

Slayed by Sunsets

Sunsets forever slay me. Big, bright, orangey ones. Peachy, pastel, soft ones. Cloudy ones and cold ones and hot summer mosquito-y night ones. Part of the reason I love them is that no photo can ever do them justice, so they are a little slice of heaven just for me at that specific moment in time. They are a reminder that life is fleeting and ever-changing.

It's difficult to pick a favorite sunset, but if I absolutely had to, I would choose Santorini, Greece. I've been fortunate enough to catch several sunsets there. The first time was in 2013 when we were on a company incentive cruise through the Adriatic Sea. James was ferociously driving me back to port on a quad to catch our ferry, but I insisted he stop off for a few minutes so we could have a photo shoot with her majesty's Mediterranean glory. I'm not sure why, but I had no pants on and was wearing a motorcycle helmet in all of the photos. The second time we caught the sunset in Santorini was on our world trip with D & B. We swam off the eighteen-flight wine tasting we had partaken in earlier that day, and then all four of us wrapped up in towels and sat on the volcanic rock to watch the sky show off.

When you keep your gaze on a sunset, it's nearly impossible to see it change. But when you turn your attention elsewhere for even a few short minutes and then look back at the sunset, it has morphed dramatically. It's hard to believe it's even the same sky you were looking at just moments before.

Personal growth works this way too. It's hard for you to notice the healthy transformation in yourself because you never look away. As a result, you don't give yourself enough credit for the growth and change you have boldly walked through. When was the last time you reflected on who you were five years ago and acknowledged how far you've come to be who you are now? It's kind of like when you lose weight. Your friends and family usually notice first. You see the numbers dropping, but it isn't until you look at your before/after pictures side-by-side that you realize how dramatic the change truly is.

There is no exact road map for personal development, but here's one thing I can tell you for sure: *everything you do matters.* And it is the actions you take when nobody is watching—choosing to read an encouraging book instead of watching TV, ordering the egg-white veggie omelet instead of the eggs benedict, re-routing a conversation instead of indulging in gossip—that matter most.

Committing to growing yourself is showing love and care for yourself. Remember, you can't help other people if you don't first help yourself.

As I mentioned, there is no concrete, predictable journey towards a more influential you, but there is a general pattern I have found to work nicely throughout my lifetime commitment to grow as a wife, friend, leader, and human.

1. Acknowledge and feed your strengths.
2. Take note of your weaknesses.
3. Identify ONE thing that is holding you back right now. A habit? A relationship? Unforgiveness towards someone? Maybe yourself?
4. Commit to ONE step you can take to overcome that one thing from Step 3.
5. Focus on that ONE step from Step 4 until Step 3 is conquered.
6. Repeat Steps 3 to 5 forever and ever.
7. Have a daily plan for expanding your mind and confidence. Podcasts, books, blogs, online communities, and so on.

**PEOPLE YOU HAVEN'T EVEN MET YET ARE
DEPENDING ON YOU TO GROW.**

Life is too short to leave your growth to chance.

 REFLECTION SECTION

In what areas of your life have you grown the last five
years?

Influence and Impact

"Did you see Angelica Lewis last night?"

"Yeah. She deserved to win."

"Yeah. Too bad it had to be *her*."

I was listening to this conversation incognito around the
corner of the hall. It was the day after the annual talent show; a
project I took under my wing to organize year after year if for no
other reason than to give myself and fellow creatives a platform to
play some live music, dance, and tell jokes. I performed a song on
the piano I wrote about my high school sweetheart and took home
the overall title for the night, so I was feeling pretty proud of myself
until I overheard this gossip session amongst two fellow classmates.

My face got hot, and my breathing got tight. How dare these band nerds talk about me in such a way! And whyyyy do people who dislike me always use my full name with such disdain?! An-gel-i-CA. My mad turned to sad fairly quickly, and I picked up my sunken ego while I sulked back to class. I never told anyone what I had heard.

Sadly, there were a handful of run-ins like this growing up. "Stuck-up" was a common adjective used to describe me. I wanted to be influential, but for so long, I thought that meant I needed to be impressive. I would try to use talent, an eye-turning wardrobe, my accolades, and newspaper features to impress people, and in turn, I believed they would follow me. I just thought that's what leaders did to inspire and impact. That's what everyone on MTV did, at least.

EVENTUALLY I LEARNED THAT TRUE LEADERSHIP IS NOT ABOUT IMPRESSING PEOPLE; IT IS ABOUT INVOLVING PEOPLE.

Leadership is simply influence, and influence is gained when people *know*, *like*, and *trust* you. Let's break each of these leadership building blocks down so that you can implement them effectively in your own life.

Know

People want to know you. They want to see your authentic self shine through. You cannot live in isolation or keep extremely private if you want to be influential. You must show up as your truest, best self every day.

For years, I believed a false idea that I had to have it all together to lead. I thought every area of my life needed to be flawless: perfect body, perfect marriage, perfect business, and perfect life. But of course, nobody is perfect. Even Beyoncé. True story. It is also not relatable. Now I don't hide challenges I'm facing. I involve my team and share how I am coming out on the other side. I no longer put on a mask of perfection, and not only is it freeing for me—it is freeing for my team. They feel more connected to me because of my transparency.

WE IMPRESS PEOPLE WITH OUR STRENGTHS BUT CONNECT THROUGH OUR WEAKNESSES.

To be more relatable, don't hide behind a mask. The real you is actually super awesome.

Like

People generally like you when you are nice to them. It's really not that complicated. Occasionally they aren't nice when you're nice to them. I speculate they must be going through a tough time. Or they are jealous of my sweet spandex. It can be hard to say.

It is in these moments that you must check your heart. Kindness is always the right thing to do, albeit it doesn't always feel like the *easiest* thing to do. I'm ashamed to admit how many people I've been unkind to. CenturyLink customer service reps. Neighbors with dogs who yap all day while the owner is at work and I'm trying to make phone calls from my home office. Prius drivers. Drivers who humdrum along below the speed limit in the left-hand lane. Passive aggressive drivers who ... OK, I'm just gonna stop right there. Just beware of driving in the PNW. I know, I KNOW! I'm certainly no finished product. There will always be room for growth. On a subconscious level, we always know what we've done.

To be more likable, put the needs of others first. And be nicer!

Trust

Building trust is fragile. And once you have it, it is so easy to lose. Many people have baggage from past relationships they carry around like a suffocating 70-pound hiker's backpack. They've been hurt, and to earn their trust will take time and thoughtfulness on your part.

The first way you build trust is through the results you've produced both for yourself and for others. People take note of your history and promise of success. Good leaders always make things happen, and results speak for themselves.

The second way you build trust is through consistency. When I share with prospects that I have been with my company for more than 10 years, it instantly heightens credibility. When I show up to appointments on time and attend every single event for my company, it displays loyalty. This is followable. Being sporadic, late, or disorganized is not.

The third way you build trust is through operating with the utmost integrity as a human being. If you are a different person behind closed doors than you are in public, you will not go far. You must set yourself apart by being exactly who you claim to be. Doing so will bring success with you everywhere you go.

TO BUILD TRUST, BE A PERSON OF YOUR WORD TO ALL COMMITMENTS.

Becoming a great leader will, undoubtedly, require you to personally grow. This is a life-long commitment. It demands that you are resolute in who you are and what you believe in. Maybe not right away, but soon enough you will see your unwavering commitment to this process show up in your relationships; how you are able to influence and impact the lives of others because of your dedication to stretch yourself to entirely new levels.

> *Life is too short to sit on the sidelines.*

REFLECTION SECTION

Who are you? What do you stand for? What do you believe in? What are your core values? What is the mission statement for your life? I've mentioned these self-reflection questions several times, but this is your friendly reminder to spend a few hours or even an entire weekend to reflect, pray, and write down what comes up for you. To take this reflection process to a deeper level, consider fasting from food while you seek clarity. When you fast, your mind becomes uncluttered and amazingly sensitive.

First Debt, Then Dog

Being a great leader requires you to live "above reproach." Meaning, operating in the highest of integrity in all that you do. One way you can do this is by *not* living above your means.

Once your initial investments have been made and your residual income is in orbit, you have to decide what to do with the extra money from this additional income stream. My recommendation is to set aside 50 percent for taxes and business expenses. And the other 50 percent? Use it to pay off any and all debt that you may have lingering.

Debt freedom is the single greatest freedom that makes all other freedoms possible. Yet 80 percent of our nation is buried in it. This includes such things as car payments, mortgages, shiny new flat screens on credit so you can see the tears stream down Tom Brady's cheekbone when he throws an interception, clothes that will be off-trend within the year, and couches and coffee tables and $42 candles. And the biggest debt culprit of all? Student loans.

I'm sorry you aren't "using" your degree and still have loans. I'm sorry you took out a $50,000 loan to get a degree only to sign the dotted line for an annual salary of $38,000. That is a bummer. But you are going to handle it, and it will no longer be a bummer. It's time to face it head on and take it down so you stop throwing your hard-earned money at interest.

IT'S WISE AND MATURE TO PAY OFF YOUR DEBT BEFORE EVER ENTERTAINING THE IDEA OF INCREASING YOUR LIFESTYLE.

Does your heart skip a beat when you see a golden-doodle? Great. Pay off your debt, and then reward yourself with a new furry friend.

Are you sick of living in a studio apartment? Great. Pay off your debt, and then add some square footage.

Is your life goal to roll dirty in an Aston Martin? Great. Pay off your debt, and then decide if it's still important to you.

Do you want to be fruitful and multiply? Great. Pay off your debt, and then make more babies.

Are you craving a vacation to Bora Bora? Great. Pay off your debt, and then spend a week in an over-the-water bungalow where you can watch stingrays swim below your glass bathroom floor while taking care of business.

The popular way to get debt-free is to go on a financial diet of sorts. To drive a beater, eat beans and rice, and deprive oneself of life's greatest pleasures, such as meeting your girlfriends for brunch. I don't believe you have to live like a college student when you are in your mid-30's to pay off debt quickly. Unless your current lifestyle is unabashedly exuberant and it's clear you should cut back, focus more on increasing your income, and not adding any additional expenses.

When James and I kicked off our marriage, neither of us had credit card debt, business debt, or student loan debt. But neither of us had a strategic plan in place for our taxes, either. From April 2013 to April 2015, we were constantly trying to play catch-up. In addition to getting ahead and proactively saving 30 to 40 percent of our income for future taxes, we had an extra $55,000 of back taxes owed from 2008 to 2010. If we didn't set out to intentionally crush this debt, we would have continued to throw money at interest for many, many more years.

We got intentional. We got focused. Two years after we said "I do," we had not only paid off that $55,000, but we got ahead of the $60,000 in the pipeline.

Here are four steps to pay off your debt with speed:

1. Get Organized

" *To whom much is given, much is required.* "

—Luke 12:48

Our very first step was to take responsibility and prepare for future abundance. Have you written down *exactly* how much debt you have? I am always shocked when I ask couples how much debt they have and they reply, "Mmmmmm, we aren't totally sure..."

Well, that's a surefire way to try and ignore a problem that will never go away. Time to get real! Go through the student loans, cars, credit cards, hospital bills, and tax liabilities, and write down the full number.

James and I each had our own accountant when we combined forces. After weighing the pros and cons, we decided to stick with mine and pull her in on our plan moving forward. She recommended we hire a bookkeeper for the ongoing organization of our expenses, city taxes, licenses, and so on. Now nearly everything is automated, and let me tell you, one of my major stresses in life has been practically eliminated.

If you are in a partnership, be sure to get organized by communicating with each other: 1) how much debt you have; 2) who is in charge of paying the bills; and 3) a timeline you'd like to be debt-free within.

2. Write a Budget

Frugal is not a word you would use to describe the Garner's. Both of us were taught never to say, "I can't afford it" and to instead say, "How can I afford it?" But we also desire to be great stewards of our money.

I roped James into doing Dave Ramsey's Financial Peace University, and we learned how to map out a budget. We discovered our cost of living was around $12,000 per month. That number included everything. All the musts—rent, food, transportation, fitness, business investments, and so on. And the fun—entertainment, clothes, beauty, travel, and so on. And of course, the percentage for giving. As Ramsey suggests, we started making cuts. We downsized our apartment and sold James' car. We didn't shop for a new fall wardrobe, and we drastically cut back on our traveling. All in all, we shaved about $2,000 per month off our expenses.

That's not gonna cut it if you want to pay off $95,000 of debt anytime in the next 50 years! However, it helped us become more in-tune with our spending habits and with each other. I still map out our budget every month to plan for our next big goals of investing into property and building our dream home.

3. Find Accountability

I'm not shy about telling friends and family about what's going on in my life—the good or bad. When people asked what was new in my life, I would say, "James and I are on a mission to pay off $55,000 debt by the end of the year, so we are super-focused right now." Or if we got invited on a getaway, I'd say, "Would love to, but our primary goal is crushing our debt, so $3,000 on a weekend trip wouldn't be in alignment with that goal at the moment."

Start speaking your goals and your vision. Let people know where you're going and why it matters to you. If you are authentic, people will respect that. And you just might inspire them in turn.

4. Add an Income Stream

Obviously, you've read this far and are well underway. This will not be an overnight process, but it can really happen much faster than you think. I prayed and prayed and prayed for provision. I prayed for a miracle. I prayed for open doors. And then went to work.

Temporary pain is worth long-term gain.

Lead from the front by choosing to become debt-free.

Life is too short to remain shackled by debt.

The Cost of Leadership

It was a balmy morning in Rio. The shutters were cracked to let in the smooth sea breeze. Jamesy and I had just finished an extravagant poolside Brazilian breakfast, complete with piles of fresh fruit, smoothies, eggs, cold cuts, bread, coffee, and tea. We were staying at a quaint and impossibly stylish luxury guesthouse in one of Rio's most exclusive neighborhoods, which was at the end of a gated street and had an ocean view that would make you question reality.

We were still basking in the festivities of the night before. The owners of this intimate gem had thrown a birthday party, and just in case this is news to you, if a gay couple who happens to own a boutique hotel in Brazil throws a party, it's going to be quite the shindig. And for some reason, probably because they knew it was going to be an all-nighter and we would complain if they didn't, they invited us. But I also think they just like to party, and so the more, the merrier.

What I can remember from that night involved many trips to the caipirinha bar, followed by getting down to Madonna on an outdoor dance floor, sneaking away with Jamesy to the rooftop deck to observe the party from up above, and then somehow ending up in a party-goer's Jeep where we found ourselves having a 2 a.m. steak dinner with seven perfect Brazilian strangers. It was a good night.

But now it was time to face reality, and that reality meant responding to an aggressive text I had received while sound asleep dreaming sweet Ipanema dreams. A leader on my team was discouraged and accusatory, so I had two choices: 1) avoid it, or 2) confront it.

Avoiding it sounded so radically appealing. Push it under a rug and hope it deals with itself. I was annoyed by the unnecessary drama, and I really just wanted to convalesce under the sun with James. And sometimes people need to work things out on their own, but in this case, I knew it needed to be confronted to be corrected. I did not want to make that call. Not one bit. I wanted to drink tropical fruit smoothies in my Brazilian bikini at our cliffside infinity pool that overlooked Sugarloaf Mountain along the Atlantic Ocean. But it is in these exact moments when we are tested. To do the hard thing, or to not do the hard thing? That is the question.

I have been fortunate to follow some of, I believe, the greatest leaders of our generation. So when I am battling a decision I ask myself, "What would my mentor do?" It's always the thing I don't want to do, of course. But here is why it is so imperative:

When you take the time to learn how to lovingly challenge, correct, and confront problematic behaviors, you show the people you care about that you actually care about them.

If you sit back and hope problems will work themselves out, you'll be disappointed to learn they generally don't. And when you're perceived as someone who doesn't really care about resolving issues, the people who look to you for leadership become disengaged. If you don't deal with problematic behavior head-on, those around you will begin to wonder where they stand as well. Over time, avoiding confrontation only multiplies the problems you need to confront.

90 minutes of painful conversation and $12 of Skype credits later, the conflict was addressed, and we had our next steps. Progress had been made instead of getting pushed under the rug. The leader was comforted, and I could go see the Christ Redeemer without a nagging feeling of irresponsibility.

Leadership is influence, and influence is the capacity to have an effect on the character, development, or behavior of someone. You grow your leadership by impacting the growth of human beings. Inspiring people with your own results is the first step to impact, but great leadership goes far beyond that.

Great leaders care. Great leaders connect. Great leaders correct. Great leaders commit.

GREAT LEADERS CONFRONT CONFLICT AND LOVINGLY KEEP THEIR FOLLOWERS ACCOUNTABLE TO THEIR VISION.

> *Life is too short to avoid the call of leadership on your life.*

REST

Does all this leadership responsibility sound like a lot of work? Well, it is. It is incredibly significant work, but it still takes a toll to be a constant source of energy for the people that follow you. That's why, it is imperative you build REST into your journey to fill up your own cup of inspiration.

Recently, I was on a leisurely walk listening to the "Enya" station on Pandora (don't knock it till you try it!), and I was amused by the variety along the local trail.

- The committed cyclists in onesies.
- The older couple with their dogs.

- The younger couples pushing strollers.
- A mom and a son holding hands.
- Techies on battery-powered skateboards and unicycles.
- The serious athletes and the weekend warriors.
- A man rowing down the river in his canoe.
- A family of three feeding the ducks.

I believe this is what is intended for a Sabbath. It doesn't have to be a Sunday, and it doesn't have to be a set thing you do or the way you rest. But it does have to delight your soul.

IN ORDER TO ENJOY THIS JOURNEY, YOU MUST FIND REST: RELAX, EXPECT, SURROUND, AND TRUST.

RELAX in the day-to-day.

Going 100 miles per hour seven days per week is not doing anyone any favors—including yourself. Yes, there are sprints of hustle when you need to dig deep to get the work done, but be sure to schedule in time to rest and balance your energy. Self-care is a part of this. I'm the queen of self-care, just ask my husband. Every day at about 4 p.m. I snuggle up and make headway on a personal development book to nourish my soul. I tackle my goals for the day, and then I give myself permission to relax my thoughts and my physical body.

But relaxing isn't just taking a nap, drawing a bath, or getting your nails done—to truly relax is to find peace amongst even the most stressful of situations. This requires tremendous discipline of the mind. It requires less striving, less busyness, and more intentionality, more belief. It requires relinquishing control to what cannot be controlled and doubling down on efforts that you can control.

EXPECT challenges.

If this journey were easy, everyone would do it! I've had people quit on me, reject me, and turn their back on me. Even my own sister joined someone else's team! The first year of growing my business, James would try to find any hole he could burrow into as to why it wasn't going to work. He even attacked the packaging of our products, and I had to let it go in one ear and out the other. He would soon understand, I had to assure myself.

My business has gone months without showing any true signs of growth. I've endured dry seasons where I feel all alone on an island, vulnerable and helpless. Sometimes challenges have felt so overbearing, I throw my hands in the air and quit. But only for a few hours. Never beyond that, because my purpose is too strong. Despite the challenges, I am able to relax and lay my head down contently at night believing I have done my best for the day, that I'm assigned to this company, I'm committed to growth, and the right people will show up at the right time.

SURROUND yourself with life-giving people.

Although James was a skeptic early on, he is now my biggest encourager and life supporter when I feel I can't move forward. I truly don't know where I would be without his positivity and belief.

As I mentioned in Chapter 2, choosing your inner circle is not a decision to be made lightly. Negativity breeds more negativity. Guard your heart by shielding yourself from nonbelievers, and keep your cup filled up by choosing positive, successful, and motivated friends.

TRUST the process.

You cannot make this journey without faith. You will never know exactly how everything is going to play out or exactly when things will happen. There will be days filled with hope and days filled with weariness and uncertainty. Get on your knees and pray for discernment and clarity. Take every single opportunity put in front of you. Hang on to your vision, and trust the process.

Your soul needs rest. If you're feeling burnt out by life's demands, then hit pause for a moment. Renew your spirit and strength by giving yourself the grace to relax and delight in this journey to become a Time Millionaire.

> *Life is too short to get too busy building a business that you forget to build your life outside of it.*

Delight and Discovery

Anyone who has been to Venice and claims they didn't get lost is lying. They are a liar.

I've been to Venice on two occasions with two different lovers. Both times, we got lost in the romance of it all. Lost because of the dead ends and old bridges and unreadable maps. Lost because all the restaurants and *tabacchis* and shoe shops start looking the same at every turn. Lost because even Google Maps is lost. But getting lost is part of the excitement! It kindles exploration. Wonder. Delight. It is quite the adventure to get lost, and nothing transports you to being fully present than finding yourself in the midst of an adventure.

My most recent visit to Venice was with Jamesy and, as per usual, we got lost. We were in Italy for only three days as we were on a Mediterranean cruise, and we simply couldn't bear the thought of getting hustled to eat at one of the establishments on the main canal with menus in four languages and waiters in tuxedo shirts. Naturally, as we were shopping around, James stumbled upon the most expensive men's boutique in Venice outside of Gucci. He fancied himself an artfully crafted jacket, and since the *Italiano* helping us out was local and stylish, we asked him where to escape the crowds to have an authentic dining experience. The recommendation was certainly off the beaten path—a sixty-euro boat ride off the beaten path—so we knew it had to be good. We shared the address with the taxi boat driver, and he gave us a surprised look. Another promising sign.

After 20 minutes or so cruising far from the crowds and into the darkness of the night, we took a sharp turn and pulled up to a scene that resembled the Pirates of the Caribbean ride at Disneyland. Groups of two and three and five hanging out on the street with their legs dangling over the water while laughing, smoking, and giving cheers. The restaurant was bustling, but we managed to find someone who spoke English enough to commandeer a small two-top for us. Then James and I did what we do best: ordered too much food and a good bottle of red to wash it down with while amusing ourselves with Venetian people watching. It was one of those nights we will never forget because we discovered something new together.

IT'S OUR SPIRITUAL NATURE TO EXPLORE BECAUSE, WITHOUT EXPLORATION, THERE'S NO DISCOVERY.

As you embark on your entrepreneurial journey, leave space for exploration and discovery. Avoid getting "destination disease." Constantly self-reflect and delight in your discovery of self. Create space for exploring new places, new people, and new ideas. Read books. Lots of books! Take chances. Travel somewhere uncomfortable. Engage in conversation with an unfamiliar face. Try a new hobby. Lead a group. Find ways to consistently challenge your comfort until you get to the point where it is actually uncomfortable for you to be comfortable.

Several times, I have heard one of my multimillionaire mentors share from the stage: "At the end of your life, you will be the culmination of three things: 1) the books you read; 2) the people you meet; and 3) the places you go."

DISCOVERY HAS THE POWER TO DELIGHT.

> *Life is too short to not enjoy it.*

 REFLECTION SECTION

What are you reading?

Who are you meeting?

Where are you going?

Finish Strong

When chasing a dream—and I've chased many—it never fails to amaze me how the unthinkable valleys hit *right* before the breakthrough. Hard stuff just keeps getting harder. The nudge to quit keeps getting louder. Distractions keep getting shinier. Self-doubt keeps getting noisier.

And then: hope.

Sometimes just a glimmer. But it's enough. Enough to remember *why* you started in the first place. Enough to stay focused on the promised outcome of fulfilling the dream instead of the disappointments.

After persevering through the long days and high altitude and squat toilets while hiking the Inca Trail, I woke up on the fourth day with hope. In just a few hours, we were going to lay eyes on Machu Picchu at sunrise AND be staying at a spa resort by nightfall! Oh, I could only imagine how it would feel to get a lavender massage and have a porcelain goddess all to myself.

But in that moment, it was 3 a.m. and blistering cold. Maybe the coldest I've ever been in my life. We had to wait several hours for the gates to open to finish the hike. Our crew was huddled together in the dark, exchanging articles of clothing to stay warm in anticipation of the four more miles and a near vertical climb that lay ahead of us in order to witness the magnificent ruins at the famed Sun Gate. *Hope* gave me the energy to finish strong.

The best part about finishing strong and fulfilling dreams is that it is rarely just about you. When you walk towards your destiny, it impacts the people around you by making deposits of inspiration into their lives.

ONE OF THE BEST WAYS YOU CAN HELP OTHERS IS BY PUSHING YOUR OWN SELF TO NEW LEVELS.

This journey is going to require hustle: the hard work you do when you don't feel like it. It is going to require long hours and saying no to some things *now* so you can say yes to more *later*. It is going to require work on your mindset like never before. To succeed, you cannot let your feelings determine your destiny, because if you run your life entirely by your emotions, you will find yourself back in that victim mindset where you allow things to happen to you instead of choosing to make things happen. You must learn how to live beyond your feelings and do what's right, even when you don't feel like it.

IT'S WORTH RISKING IT ALL BECAUSE OF THE JOY AND FREEDOM THAT COME.

> *Life is too short to choose the pain of regret over the pain of discipline.*

Living Your Legacy

As I wrap up this book, precious little Sofia Grace Garner is growing inside my belly. Admittedly, I have never been more grateful to be a Time Millionaire as I manage bouts of fatigue and exhaustion (you mommas know what I'm talking about!). I have spent many days of this pregnancy wrapped up on our couch in a fuzzy blanket, reflecting on the legacy James and I hope to create and the impact we are working to make. You see, the decision to be a Time Millionaire is only about you and your goals at the very beginning. By sticking and staying, it soon becomes a butterfly effect that impacts many people in your life, and perhaps even generations to come.

I want you to picture for a moment, many years down the road, you are sitting in a rocking chair on your front porch. You are gazing out at the flowers and trees and bees buzzing in your front yard. You take a deep breath with your eyes closed to embrace the smells of nature around you. Your loved ones are inside the home beyond the screen door, clanking plates and talking with laughter, and you are thinking either one of two things:

1. "I wonder what would've happened if we had done that thing..."

OR

2. "Wow. I can't imagine if we hadn't done that thing. Look at all the blessings that have come because we chose the road less traveled. The decision to become a Time Millionaire has filled our lives with unspeakable joy and wonder."

Which scenario sounds better to you?

I have this fantasy that James and I will die holding hands in bed like the old couple in *Titanic*. It may sound morbid, but we actually do discuss death quite frequently. It keeps reality in our faces and allows us to operate with a healthy respect for the brevity of life. That nothing is guaranteed, and nothing lasts forever. I don't know how much longer we have, but I do know we will go to the grave fighting for these three things:

1. The future of our family.

2. The legacy we want to leave.

3. The difference we want to make.

Life is short, and happiness is simple: Love unconditionally, find compassion by listening to someone's story and offering what you can to help, and do stuff that's hard even when you don't feel like it. And by all means, break bread with people and have a good laugh.

It's time for you to rise and shine, Champion. It's time for you to step into your destiny and do whatever it takes to earn your freedom. Someone is counting on you. The greatest things we leave behind are the deposits we make on others. Become a Time Millionaire so that you can be available for people.

TO LEAVE A LEGACY, YOU MUST START LIVING A LEGACY.

Life is too short to not live it to the fullest.

YOUR NEXT STEPS

Above all, I pray this book has given you hope. Hope for a better future. Hope to start filling your days with more stuff that matters. Hope to experience complete financial freedom. Hope to live out your most epic story. Now that you have the success principles I've laid out here, you have everything you need to #HustleSmarter with network marketing by applying the ultimate strategy: work hard and pray hard. Work harder on yourself than anything else. Believe big and stretch your faith to entirely new levels.

I shared in these pages only the exercises and strategies that have been proven to work in my own and other team's businesses. You can walk in complete confidence knowing you're implementing a plan that has been proven.

Once you have written responses in your journal to all *Reflection Sections*, here is what I'd recommend for next steps:

1 If you aren't already a distributor, choose a company to align with and sign up at whatever level will position you as a business builder.

Still unsure which company best suits your values? Sign up for my free #HustleSmarter webinar at [www.hustlesmarterwebinar.com] to learn more about the company I am an Independent Distributor for and how you can join my team to work with me directly.

2 Make your list and have your story ready to share whenever the opportunity presents itself to make an impact. You cannot run your business without these two things. Your list is your working capital; it employs you every day. Your story is your message and is how you will communicate the benefits of your products and opportunity to your list.

3 Connect with your upline mentor. Schedule a time to talk and ask their advice on how they think you can personally and professionally grow. This may be a tough conversation, but it is very possible they see something holding you back that you can't see. Trust their experience. Trust the process. Great leaders are first great followers.

4 Go change the world with your products and opportunity. Integrate the products into your daily life and allow them to change you for the better. Be an incredible coach and help your customers get life-changing results regardless of what industry you are in. Follow up and follow through.

5   Give this book to anyone you know who needs hope. Anyone who needs more time, more energy, and more money for the things they love. Network marketing could change everything for them.

I'm so grateful for you.
YOU are a Champion.
Make your life epic.
And #HustleSmarter.

— Ang

ACKNOWLEDGEMENTS

To my Sweet Jamesy. I wake up every day in complete awe that God gifted me with the most perfect puzzle piece. You are an incredible husband with an incredible heart and an incredible ability to encourage me in my dreams. I love sharing triumphs with you. I love sharing challenges with you. I love doing life with you. Thank you for your bottomless support and willingness to speak truth and love into my life.

To Mom and Dad. You gave me the freedom and independence to become the best me, and for that I am forever grateful. Mom, thank you for loving me unconditionally and encouraging me to use my voice for God's glory. Dad, thank you for lavishly blessing me with everything I have ever needed to chase my dreams. I love you both so very much.

To Charlie Ragus and the Ragus family. Thank you for your vision and fight to create a business opportunity that stands in the highest of integrity, providing freedom for so many families across America.

To Mike and Janelle Friedrich. Thank you for believing in me, following up with me, loving on me, and being patient with me.

When I walk into your home, I feel as though someone has wrapped me in a blanket of peace. Thank you for providing a safe environment to grow. The impact you have made on James and I will surely have a ripple effect on our children and our children's children.

To Rick Loy, Ron Reynolds, Debra Fisser, Bob and Jenny Donnelly, Diane and Danny McDaniel, Kristi McGihon, Karen Edwards, Wayne Johnson, Richard and Sherry Wright, and Nate and Jen DeTracy. Thank you for leading the way. Thank you for setting the bar. Thank you for exemplifying the highest of character in all that you do. The words you have spoken have changed my life forever and influenced much of this book.

To Stephanie and John Grandits, Stephanie and Jesse Doyle, Jessie Christensen, and all of the leaders on our team. Thank you for saying YES to locking arms with us and answering the call of leadership on your lives.

To D & B. How fortunate are James and I to have friends like you who accept us when we are at our lowest and champion us when we are at our highest. We are blessed to know and grow with you. Love you.

To my amazing launch team. Because of you, many more people have the vision and tools to forge towards a life with more impact and meaning and time for the things they love.

ABOUT THE AUTHOR

Angie Garner is a fitness expert, nutrition coach, and developer of leaders. She started her first personal training business at age 21, opened a gym in Seattle by the age of 23, and now puts her heart and soul into mentoring her AdvoCare team across the nation. She is also the creator and host of the #HustleSmarter Podcast, a lifelong resident of the Pacific Northwest, and her best role of all: Wife of Sweet Jamesy. In 2016, they put their belongings in storage and traveled for eight months across five continents, returning home with a deeper desire to help people get financially and physically free.

You can find out more and connect with her at
www.angiegarner.com.

TIME MILLIONAIRE RESOURCES

PODCAST
HustleSmarter with Angie Garner

EMAIL
hello@angiegarner.com

FACEBOOK
www.facebook.com/angie.lewis

INSTAGRAM
@angie.garner

FREE BUSINESS TRAINING
www.hustlesmarterwebinar.com

FREE NUTRITION TRAINING
www.nutrition101webinar.com

FREE MINDSET CHALLENGE
www.mindsweatreset.com